On the Bus

Four Buses,
Forty Years, and
400,000 miles

Sacramento, California

On The Bus

**Four Buses,
Forty Years, and
400,000 miles**

John LaTorre

Sacramento, California

© 2016, by John LaTorre

ISBN-13: 978-0-9790635-1-0

John LaTorre
Library of Congress Cataloging-in-Publication Data

LaTorre, John, 1948-
    On the Bus

Disclaimer: We note that model names, designations, etc. are the property of the trademark holder, and are mentioned for identification purposes only. This book is not an official publication.

Sacramento, California

Table of Contents

Introduction

With two exceptions, books about Volkswagen buses seem to fall into three categories.

First, there are the repair manuals that describe, in dry detail, the steps required to perform certain repairs. They are typically illustrated with black-and-white photographs of perfectly clean engines being worked on by professional technicians dressed in impossibly spotless smocks.

Then there are the automotive histories. Some of them give the company's history from its somewhat suspect origins in Nazi Germany to its present status as one of the world's greatest carmakers. Others, written mostly for the collectors, enumerate the specifications of the various models down the years. If these have pictures, they are there to illustrate the differences between one model and the next, from window shapes to door handles to suspensions to paint schemes, in obsessive detail.

Finally, you have the books written by devotees who enthuse about the car's mystique and how it changed transportation forever and so on. These books are often illustrated profusely with full-color pictures of faultless restorations, wacky paint jobs, and snapshots taken at any of a number of conventions and meetings of similar Volkwagen devotees. It's obvious that the writers love their buses beyond all reason.

The first exception to these three genres of books is John Muir's *How to Keep Your Volkswagen Alive*, a book so radical in its concept and execution that it deserves a chapter of its own, and it gets one in this book. It was written by an engineer who found much to love in the car, and much to disparage. He wanted to write a repair manual that could be used by anybody regardless of automotive training or mechanical ability and, for the most part, he succeeded. But his message was really about empowerment and self-reliance. It was more "know thyself" than "know thy car" and, in that sense, it was like no other repair book ever written. Until it came out, there was nothing quite like it. Now there are thousands of "Dummy" or "Idiot" self-help books written from the same perspective of the expert speaking to the novice.

The second exception is this book.

Frankly, I'm not sure what kind of a book this is. In parts, it's a travelogue, by somebody who doesn't particularly like to travel. It's a mechanic's log, from a non-mechanic who hates to get his hands dirty. And it's a history, from somebody who never had much interest in history. It might be best summed up as a coming-of-age story about a man whose life came to be shaped by a vehicle that he happened upon almost by chance.

I guess you could say that I'm a fan of the Volkswagen bus. I've owned four of them, and logged a total of a close to a half a million miles driving them all over the United States, most recently in California and the American Southwest. I've come to admire the excellence of its engineering and the ruggedness of its construction (the latter of which I've tested on untold miles of undeveloped roads, or no roads at all), and the huge variety of uses it has been put to. There will be stories about that here in the book. At the same time, I've been frustrated by some of the shortcomings of that same design, and had my share of breakdowns on the road. There are stories of that, too. I've driven my buses hard and taken the consequences. If you're looking for a paean to the Transporter, this is not that book.

With the obvious exception of the Muir book, most of the others have been written by people who have driven buses, sometimes for astounding distances, but may not have spent much time under the hood, so to speak. I have a different perspective. I've done just about every procedure in Muir's book, including dismantling engines down to the crankshaft and rebuilding them, not once but several times. Brake jobs? Done several. Wheel bearings? Ditto. Generator overhauls? Yup. Constant velocity joints? God, what a mess that was! Mufflers? More than I care to count. Tune-ups? Hundreds of them. Re-upholstering? Not much, but some. So you're reading a book by a man who has had a bit of dirt, grease, and experience under his fingernails.

Although this book has been, in a sense, gestating for over forty years, the impetus for getting it done was a camping trip I took in my Toyota Sienna. Now the Sienna is a wonderful vehicle. It is everything the bus is not: mechanically reliable, steady on the highway, and easy to drive for long distances at freeway speeds in air-conditioned comfort. But I found that as a camper, it didn't hold a candle to the VW buses I've owned. I missed the spaciousness of the bus's interior, that pop-up top that gave me standing room, the numerous storage compartments, the double-size bed, the cooking and washing areas, and much more. My wife had largely given up camping, since the effort of setting up camp and breaking it down again had taken much of the fun out of it. I thought that the ease of camping with a Westfalia camper would be the way to get her back into it. As it turned out, I was wrong about that, but I re-discovered the fun of camping in the bus. If you suggested to me that what I was really enjoying was a re-discovery of the younger man that I had once been, I would not be inclined to argue with you.

It's one thing to reminisce about the Good Old Days. It's another thing to re-explore them, but that was what I wanted to do. And the only way to do that was to buy another camper. In fact, I would buy a camper in some need of restoration, rebuild it, and write about the experience! If all went well, I could own a Westfalia camper without spending a ton of money, have some stories to tell, and even make a buck or two off the process. It is of such harebrained schemes that adventures are made.

What follows are some experiences I've had with the bus I own now and its three predecessors, interspersed with ruminations on the history of the Transporter and other topics of interest to those who also admire this unique vehicle. I've tried to tell the truth to the best of my memory, but memory is a slippery beast, and sometimes plays tricks. My latest bus has been reminding me of many things I'd forgotten: the smell of warm engine oil that seems to permeate every bus I've owned, the drone of the engine as the miles roll by and the bus sings its song of the road. Antoine de Saint-Exupéry talked about many of those things in the fine books he wrote on flying piston-engine airplanes in the 1930s, but the VW bus owner knows them firsthand. Saint-Exupèry also knew that the secret of flying in turbulence is to use lots of small, quick corrections instead of

3

large, slow ones, and to beware of crosswinds. VW bus drivers know about that, too. Aviators and VW bus drivers have more in common than it appears at first glance, and it comes as no surprise to find how many hang glider pilots, instructors, and designers have owned a bus at some time or other. I was one of them.

PART ONE: Before George

The Anti-Classic Car

The Volkswagen bus is an affront to classic cars everywhere. *Classic cars are supposed to be sleek.* The bus has all the elegance of a rural mailbox. Even the advertising people who were responsible for selling it would apologize for its looks and direct your attention to its practicality instead. *Classic cars are supposed to be powerful and roadworthy.* The bus accelerates like it's towing a trailer twice its weight, and while in most conditions it's well-behaved, a moderate crosswind can push it around with impunity, forcing the driver to keep a firm hand on the wheel.

Classic cars are supposed to be ahead of their time technologically. While the bus had a few design elements that were uncommon on commercial vehicles at the time (and even today), it's a car that stubbornly resisted improvement. It didn't have a twelve-volt electrical system until the mid-sixties, a decade after it became standard on American cars. It didn't have an automatic transmission until the seventies, and it never really had air conditioning worth the name until Volkswagen rolled out the Vanagon in 1980. Its heater was so feeble that customers in northern climes readily sprang for an optional gasoline-fired heater, at considerable extra cost. Roll-down windows and a single-piece windshield weren't added until 1968, almost twenty years after they became standard equipment on American trucks. And it stayed with air-cooled engines up until the mid-eighties, long after most other manufacturers had discarded them in favor of water-cooled engines.

Classic cars are usually born of a designer's dream, and are expected to express his or her vision of what the ultimate car should be like. The bus's designers had a different objective: to make a vehicle that could carry the most payload for its size, in the most economical way, at the expense of nearly every feature that most cars take for granted: comfort, convenience, and performance. A gas gauge? You won't get one, because you don't need one. A small reserve tank is all you need, and that's what you'll get. If you can't remember to keep it filled, you don't deserve to drive a bus. A powerful engine? Don't be silly. You'll get the same engine we put in the Beetle, and you'll like it.

And yet even thirty-year-old buses are selling for more than what they cost originally, and the original split-window buses can go for what a new car costs today ... if you can find them. You can easily spend twenty grand on one that's not close to being in running condition. And, unlike most cars of the fifties and sixties and seventies, an amazing number of them are still on the road, a fair number of them as "daily drivers" (an automotive term for cars that are used every day as one's basic means of transport).

They have never asked to be babied. A little routine maintenance every three thousand miles or so, and they'll soldier on through good weather and bad, on roads that scarcely deserve the name. They don't use much gas or oil. They don't use coolant at all. They don't like hills, but if you have the time, they'll get you over them, in first or second gear all the way. If you break down, parts are still available (although their quality can be dodgy) and there are still mechanics who understand how different these cars are from everything else on the road. Owners are still advised to keep repair manuals and factory service manuals on board, just in case. Astonishingly, these are still in print, even after a half a century. And it's a rare owner that doesn't travel far without a spare fan belt, fuses, valve cover gaskets, and a basic tool kit.

In short, this car breaks all the rules of classic car ownership and appreciation, and still finds more than its fair share of aficionados. All over the world, there are special events and shows that draw hundreds or even thousands of buses from far and near, far more than any other car marques of the era. And for every bus, there seem to be a hundred baby boomers with fond memories of a youth misspent in and around them, memories that have somehow shouldered out the memories of breakdowns and freezing winters and all the drawbacks of bus ownership. It has emerged as an enduring symbol of their youth, of limitless horizons and quirky individualism, of forging one's own way against the tide of conformity and societal expectations and ... well, against middle age.

Not bad for a vehicle that was designed as a cheap way to deliver packages and equipment in an economy recovering from the wreckage of war. Not bad at all.

Prologue – Concerning Buses

The Volkwagen Bus, also called the Transporter or the Type II (to distinguish it from its older brother the Beetle, which was the Type I), began life as a sketch by a VW salesman named Ben Pon. Pon was a Dutchman who was primarily responsible for opening export markets for the infant Volkswagen company, which was formed after World War II on what was left of the war-ravaged factory and staff that Nazi Germany had set up to produce the "people's car." He became the company's leading exporter, setting up a distributorship in the Netherlands that became one of that country's great post-war success stories. Having successfully sold Volkswagens to the Dutch, who had suffered greatly under German occupation during the war, Pon had the reputation of being able to sell anything to anybody, but his attempt to bring the unconventional Beetle to the United States in 1949 was an utter failure. Others would later succeed beyond all expectations, of course, but Pon had already made his own mark on the future of the company with a crude drawing he made sometime around 1947.

The story goes that on one of his trips to the factory, he noticed a curious parts mover called the *plattenwagen* or "flatcar." It used the chassis of a VW jeep with a rudimentary driver's cab over the rear wheels. All the space in front of him was dedicated to a platform that was used for transporting parts around the factory. This vehicle was the brainchild of Major Ivan Hurst, a British officer who was managing the Volkswagen factory while the Occupation authorities were trying to figure out what to do with it. Pons made a sketch of a commercial van which was based on that concept, but which put the driver over the front wheels, and showed it to Major Hurst. By most accounts, Hurst wasn't interested.[1]

---

[1] One writer, Laurence Meredith, maintains that it wasn't Hurst who put the kibosh on the idea, but a superior officer, Colonel Charles Radclyffe, whose permission was needed before money could be spent on the project. Radclyffe maintained that while the idea was intriguing, the Volkswagen plant was too undercapitalized at that point to consider bringing out new products. He deemed it wiser to devote the Beetle's

But Pon's sketch eventually found its way onto the desk of Heinz Nordhoff, the chief executive officer who replaced Hurst at the company. During World War II, Nordhoff had managed Europe's largest commercial truck factory for Opel in Brandenburg, and he knew a thing or two about trucks and the commercial vehicle market. Although he was producing Ferdinand Porsche's Beetle design by the thousands, he was looking for a design he could put his own stamp on, and the "transporter" seemed to fit the bill. He knew that Germany needed a vehicle that could be used to help clear away the rubble of the late war, deliver new building materials to rebuild the cities, and transport consumer goods that the recovering economy was starting to demand. Maybe there's a market for these things, he thought. He gave Alfred Häsner, one of his designers, a year to put one into production.

For the engine, Häsner used the only engine VW had, which was the beetle's four-cylinder air-cooled engine. People have usually given Porsche the credit for this engine, but this was accurate only in the most general sense. It is true that Porsche listed the basic design and specifications that the engine was to have, but the actual plans and engineering were done by Franz Xaver Reimspeiss, who was one of Porsche's top engineers. (Reimspeiss's design was based on an earlier engine that Josef Kales, another Porsche associate, had made for a Volkswagen prototype that NSU commissioned but never produced commercially.) Although such engines had existed before in cars and airplanes, Reimspeiss's version advanced the concept dramatically. He gave it an effective cooling system using air forced in by a blower that ran off the generator; in fact, the generator and fan shared a common axle connected to the crankshaft by a fan belt. The engine was lighter than most engines of that displacement, but it was robust, having been engineered so that none of its parts were operating near their failure limits. It was designed to operate best when at its highest revolutions per minute, and to run at that speed indefinitely.

---

profits into refining the car and promoting it rather than to develop a new line of automobile.

Best of all, it could be easily modified. The major components were simply bolted together, making disassembly and re-fitting of parts easy. As racing aficionados found out how simple it was to tinker with, an entire industry sprang up to provide them with larger cylinders and pistons and modified crankshafts and camshafts, and Formula V racing was born. In fact, modifying and racing Volkswagens was a popular pastime in post-war Europe, since military surplus Kübelwagens (or "bucket-cars," Germany's answer to the American jeeps) were abundant, rugged, and cheap.

Volkswagen never endorsed these modifications, since they could shorten engine life, but it took advantage of what was learned and, over the next thirty years, gradually doubled the engine's displacement until its theoretical limits had at last been reached. So effective and versatile was this engine that it ended up being used for static motors and light aircraft, including versions of the revolutionary Horten flying wing, a design forty years ahead of its time. The engine's basic design wouldn't be drastically altered until flatter versions of it were developed in the 1960s to fit it into the lower engine bays of the later buses, squarebacks, and 411 sedans that VW was designing. (The latter two were intended to replace the Beetle, but never caught on.) Reimspeiss's engine eventually succumbed not so much to demands for increased power but to emission-control laws; it became harder and harder to hang the necessary smog equipment on it. It was clear that the future lay with water-cooled engines, and all VW models from the eighties onward had them, except for the beetles that continued to be manufactured and sold in Mexico and South America until around the turn of the century. By that time, millions and millions of Reimspeiss's engine had been made, in plants all over the world, both as original equipment and for replacement parts. It could be argued that this engine was the most popular automotive engine design of all time, going into not only countless beetles, dune buggies and buses, but a plethora of military vehicles, airplanes, and specialty cars like the Thing.

Häsner's initial design for the bus called for a boxy body sitting atop a Beetle chassis. By putting the driver and a passenger into seats over the front wheels, he reasoned, he could balance their weight in the front with the engine and transmission's weight over the rear wheels, resulting in a weight distribution that wouldn't change much whether the van was empty or loaded. He would use a body welded to the beetle's corrugated-steel floor pan, keeping production costs to a minimum.

Then came the tests. The flat face of the van created so much wind resistance that the poor little engine was overloaded at anything approaching highway speed. A series of tests in wind tunnels (possibly the first ones ever conducted for commercial vehicles) dictated a re-design to a rounded, sloping front and rounded rear corners, dropping the coefficient of drag from 0.75 to 0.43. (By comparison, the Beetle's drag coefficient was around 0.48.) Now the van could get up to highway speeds.

The only other serious hitch was when the floor pan in the prototype kept cracking. Häsner's team realized that they'd need to use a more conventional ladder-frame construction using two parallel steel girders connected with cross-braces. It was not an easy decision, because this design would increase the weight of the vehicle and greatly reduce the acceleration that the already over-taxed engine could achieve, but there was no alternative. They made the changes, and the prototype was ready to be revealed on November 11, 1949, a year and a day after Häsner started recruiting his design team.

Häsner left VW shortly thereafter; from the surviving accounts, it's unclear whether Volkswagen forced him out, citing the many setbacks in the bus's design process, or whether he himself was dissatisfied with the final product (in particular, he felt that the proper place for an engine was in the front of the car, not the rear). At any rate, he found a job with Ford of Germany, designing a van for them called the FK (for Ford Köln) 1000. On the outside, it was startlingly similar to the bus, even to the rounded front and split windshield, but sported a radiator between the headlights. On the inside, Häsner used a conventional front-engine/rear-wheel-drive drive train with the drive shaft under the floor, allowing the cargo area to be perfectly flat all the way to the rear door. Later renamed the Ford Transit, it would become one of Europe's most popular commercial vehicles and, like the bus, its descendents remain in production today. It was, in fact, the template for most of the vans that other manufacturers were making in the sixties and seventies under names like the Ford Econoline and the GMC Handivan.

Häsner's basic design for the bus was so sound that it wasn't changed for nearly twenty years. That design included using as many of the Beetle's body and trim parts as it could. Almost all of the electrical components except for the wiring harnesses themselves could be interchanged. The two models shared a host of trim features; even the headlight bezels were the same. The idea was to keep the required inventory of spare parts to an absolute minimum, and to lower the cost of each part through mass production.

The motoring press took quickly to this unconventional design. Here was the truck that Germany had been waiting for — capacious, frugal with gas, with easy and responsive handling. For a truck, it was even fun to drive, and the owner's manual warned against the temptation to drive it at speeds greater than it was designed to handle. It shared with the Beetle an engine that required no coolant, could operate at close to top speed for extended periods, and was easy to repair or, in a matter of minutes, to switch out entirely for a rebuilt engine. The large cargo space virtually cried out for customization, a blank canvas begging for an artist to adorn it. But the best thing the bus had going for it was its uniqueness. In its class, there was simply no competition, and there wouldn't be any for years.

Nordhoff's analysis was right on the money; there was indeed a market for these strange beasts. The first Transporters rolled off the assembly line in 1949; within ten years, it was the best-selling commercial vehicle in Germany. It could be had in a variety of interior styles, from straight cargo vans to eleven-passenger buses, hearses, ambulances, fire trucks, and campers. It was your basic "box with a motor," small on the outside (only a hand-span longer than the VW Beetle) and cavernous on the inside. It had an extra pair of gear boxes that sat above and just inside of the rear wheels, giving a lowered gear ratio and a higher ground clearance. These "transfer cases"

13

had been originally developed during World War II for the *Kübelwagen* to give Porsche's original Beetle design more off-road capability and low-end torque, and they would later turn up on an updated version of that military vehicle, marketed as a fun car called the Trekker or the Safari everywhere in the world but the U.S., where General Motors had already used that name for a Pontiac station wagon. For unfathomable reasons, Volkswagen renamed it the "Thing" for the American market.

Although VW buses, like other models of foreign cars, were sporadically brought into the U.S by returning servicemen, businessmen, and tourists in the early 1950s, they weren't officially imported by VW dealers until around 1954 (the same year that Nordhoff decided to build a new factory to produce nothing but buses). It was, in many ways, a tough sell. Just as there had been no car like the Beetle on American roads, these odd-shaped vans were completely alien to the American car-buyer. Compared to even the most anemic American cars, they were horribly underpowered. They were unpleasant to drive in crosswinds. Their air-cooled engines made a frightful racket. There were no automatic transmissions, no air conditioners, no power brakes and no power steering. It didn't even have a fuel gauge; instead, you got a little reserve tank under the front seat that was filled from the main tank. If you remembered to flip the lever that closed the passageway between the tanks after you filled the main tank, you had an extra gallon to get to the next gas station on. If you didn't remember, you were out of luck, because the reserve tank would go dry when the main tank did.

But they gave a lot of cargo-carrying capacity for their size and could be adapted to many of the same uses that their overseas brothers were performing, and these virtues convinced a lot of people to buy them despite their drawbacks. By the nineteen-sixties, they were being used all over the country in places like cities, farms and ranches, where top speeds didn't matter much and their particular virtues of small size (in the city) or off-road capability (on the farm or the ranch) could be appreciated. One of the bus's outstanding traits was its traction in soft ground, due to its placement of the engine and transmission over the drive wheels, rather than over the steering

14

wheels. With that feature, VW bypassed a common fault of light vans and trucks, a fault I became personally acquainted with when I owned a small Toyota pickup. That beast never handled well unless it had a few hundred pounds of cargo on the bed. But my buses handled about the same whether empty or loaded, and seldom got stuck traversing terrain that would have given pause to most small trucks or passenger cars.

Another thing that sold the Volkswagen was its superlative service network. Even before dealerships were established in an area, parts were warehoused in strategic locations and mechanics were trained to service them. A high ratio of mechanics (and of service bays) to car sales was dictated by the company, and strictly adhered to by the dealers as a condition of their contracts. This, too, showed the hand of Nordhoff, who used to write service manuals for Opel and who, after World War Two, worked as the chief mechanic of a car repair shop — the only job the erstwhile manager of Europe's largest truck factory could obtain. He vowed never to sell a Volkswagen in any part of the world where service wasn't already available. [2]

VW also benefited from one of the great advertising campaigns of the 1960s. These ads were composed by New York's Doyle Dane Bernbach agency and glorified the simplicity, engineering and value of the Beetle in a series of award-winning, self-deprecating ads. At first, the VW bus was handled by another agency more adept at appealing to the truck market, since they were basically marketed as cargo vans. But in 1964, a 25% increase in imported truck tariffs almost killed the sales of VW Transporters, which were already priced at a lower profit margin to better compete with American trucks. Sales plummeted.

VW's solution to the problem was to reposition the Transporter as a "station wagon" with three rows of seats,

---

[2] It is intriguing to speculate that having actually had grease under his nails put Nordhoff in a unique position to understand how important the mechanic was in the scheme of things. I suspect things were different at Renault, to name one manufacturer, as I found when I had to change a dash light bulb in my R16, a task that ended up taking five hours ("Step One: Remove steering wheel. Step Two: remove dash board, unplugging and labeling every single wire that connected to it," and so on).

15

thereby evading the truck tariff. (VW had been providing buses with such people-carrying capabilities almost from the day the bus was introduced.) In effect, VW had invented the minivan, twenty years before the term itself was coined. As a station wagon, it was marketed to an entirely different set of people than it had been offered to as a truck, and Doyle Dane Bernbach started producing ads for the station wagon as well as the Beetle. (Detroit has shown itself equally adept at repositioning vehicles to take advantage of breaks given to one class of vehicle; for years, they've been selling "Sports-Utility Vehicles" to the mass market as consumer vehicles while classifying them as trucks with the federal government, to evade the higher mileage and emissions standards required of passenger cars.)

By the mid-sixties, Transporters came to be identified as "hippie buses" favored by the counter-culture of the time, to the dismay of the hard-nosed businessmen of Volkswagen of America. Nomadic and iconoclastic by nature, the counter-culture found a lot to admire in the bus's idiosyncratic design and proceeded to claim it as its own. (In large part, it was because you could buy them for peanuts, as the original owners traded up to the more powerful American vans that were becoming available.) In "Alice's Restaurant," one of 1968's landmark recordings, Arlo Guthrie sang of using "a red VW Microbus" to haul a half a ton of garbage from a friend's home in an ill-fated mission of friendship. In 1969, a former engineer turned drop-out named John Muir put out a self-published book called *How to Keep Your Volkswagen Alive,* about which we'll hear more of later on. And in 1971, Gurney Norman wrote a book about some sixties-era stoners that was narrated by a VW bus named Urge. The novel, called *Divine Right's Trip,* would be printed in its entirety within the pages of the Portola Institute's *Last Whole Earth Catalog,* a publication often described as the "Sears catalog of the Counterculture." The VW bus became so iconic of that era and culture that, thirty years later, all an advertising company needed to invoke it was a picture of a VW bus painted with flowers and peace signs, sitting in a field. And when Jerry Garcia of the Grateful Dead died, a VW ad showed a drawing of a split-face VW bus shedding a tear from its left headlight. The ad marked not only the passing of a rock icon but of a sea change in the attitude of Volkswagen's management. It is perhaps not coincidental that VW was then on the verge of introducing the New Beetle, another attempt to cash in on the nostalgia for the sixties.

I came to know three subsets of bus aficionados personally in the 1970s and 1980s. First came the camping crowd, who found these little boxes ideal as rolling campsites. The Volkswagen company was quick to recognize the potential of this market, and it licensed coachmakers like Germany's Westfalia and England's Dormobile to outfit special versions of the bus with raiseable roofs, a rear bench seat that converted into a double bed, a water reservoir with a pump-operated spigot, an icebox, lots of cabinets and storage nooks and, later on, refrigerators and stoves. If you needed more space, you could arrange for hammocks or cots in the expanded roof area or buy a tent that attached to the side of the camper. It was simplicity itself. While your fellow campers spent an hour setting up their tents and tables and cooking areas and what-not, you simply rolled into the site, raised the roof, flipped the bed down, and you were done. Owners who were also skilled woodworkers and tinkerers found that the interior space of an unadorned cargo van positively cried out for modification and created their own campers, which ranged in quality from crude platforms and cabinets (or even a simple mattress thrown over the floor) to compact, intricately designed interiors that a yacht builder would have envied.

Next came the surfers, who found the bus handy for carrying surfboards in the ten-foot cargo area. Let a little air out of the tires, and they could drive them right onto the beach, relying on the weight of the engine to give the rear wheels some traction.

Last came hang glider pilots, who would load their gliders on roof racks and take advantage of the bus's ability to scramble up slopes that would have daunted more conventional cars and trucks. Many of these sportsmen and sportswomen, seeking the remoteness of faraway mountaintops, found that a camper with a roof rack fitted their life-styles perfectly. Here's a snapshot, taken around 1990, of three VW campers lined up in a row

17

outside the factory of Pacific Airwave, one of the major hang glider makers at the time. All of them were owned by employees of the company, each of whom was also a hang glider pilot.

Three buses lined up at Pacific Airwave

The one on the left was mine.

Not everybody loved the Transporter. Consumers Union (CU), a nonprofit testing organization, would routinely fail the car as "Unacceptable" in its *Consumer Reports* magazine. This was due mainly to the car's sluggishness at reaching freeway and passing speeds and for its susceptibility to crosswinds and gusts. The Center for Auto Safety (CAS), a group founded by consumer advocate Ralph Nader and staffers from the non-profit Consumers Union, went even further. Its book *Small — on Safety*, called the Volkswagen Microbus "…by a wide margin the most dangerous four-wheel vehicle *of any type* designed for highway use and sold in significant numbers." (The italics are theirs.) It found the bus even more dangerous than the VW Beetle, which it called "the most hazardous car currently in use in significant numbers in the United States" and claimed that it had twice the fatality rate of American-built cars. To the list of shortcomings that the CAS documented in the Beetle's design (among them, severe handling problems and minimal crash protection), they added the lack of what it called "crush distance" … the distance the front of the vehicle could collapse in a front-end collision before the front-seat occupants were affected. (The bus did come out ahead of the bug, though, in the security of its

18

fuel tank in a crash.) While the CAS proposed many retrofits to the Beetle to increase its safety, they felt that the bus was essentially unfixable, and called on Volkswagen to recall each and every one of them and to recompense their owners.

These evaluations have merit; when measured by the benchmarks that CU regularly used on all cars of that era, the bus came up short. But the condemnations from Consumers Union and the Center for Auto Safety have been bitterly contested by bus lovers. They protest that the bus was being compared to the conventional American station wagons, and that greater weight should have been given to the bus's load-carrying capacity and its greater reliability. (On one of the VW discussion groups I subscribe to, several people commented on CU's recommendation of a 1971 GMC Suburban as a better choice; one of them asked how many of those 1971 Suburbans — or any cars of that era — are still in daily use on the road today.)

My own feeling is that they were right to warn people about how the bus differed from the cars of that era. In many ways (and for many of the same reasons), their situation resembled that of sport-utility vehicles in the last part of the twentieth century. Although they weren't really cars, and didn't handle like cars, they were sold to people who didn't know how different they were from the sedans they were already driving.

Tom and Ray Magliozzi, in their book *Car Talk*, made this point when they were discussing the four-wheel-drive utility vehicles of that era. With tongue in cheek, they proposed a warning label for the dashboard that said: "WARNING! THIS IS NOT A CAR. DON'T DRIVE IT LIKE A CAR OR YOU WILL SURELY DIE." The Magliozzi brothers have professed no great love for the VW bus, listing it as among the top ten scariest vehicles and calling it "probably one of THE least safe vehicles in existence" on their web site. So we can assume that they would not have objected to the installation of this warning placard on buses as well.

During the eighties, Volkswagen created a series of ads using the German word "Fahrvegnügen," meaning "enjoyment of driving." Those of us who drove buses, and knew a little German, would change this to "Gefahrvegnügen," or "enjoyment of danger," in wry acknowledgement of the risks of driving them.

19

The bus was definitely not a car that invited comparison to American iron; it was pitifully underpowered compared to American cars and trucks. Even the grades along freeways that failed to bother most cars would daunt the bus, forcing the driver to downshift to third or even second gear to make the slope. And it would never be the vehicle of choice for those who needed to get there in a hurry; the cruising speed of even the later ones was no more than a comfortable sixty or so, on level ground with no headwind. Sixty-five could be done, but at the cost of increased engine wear, so that speed was reserved for the passing lanes.[3] Beyond that, the wind resistance of that big slab face overpowered the engine's meager output. You could stand on the accelerator pedal, but it wouldn't make any difference.

As a result, people who drove VW buses a lot tended to be better than average drivers. They had to be. A VW bus driver had to pay constant attention to the road and to traffic. Without the ability to accelerate quickly, special care had to be taken when changing lanes or merging onto freeways. You had to take into account not only the rates of speed of the traffic around you but the terrain you were encountering, because an uphill stretch could cause you to lose speed just when you needed to make a lane change. There was an on-ramp on the Jones Falls Expressway in Baltimore that filled me with dread, because it was a long uphill pull that resulted in the shortest merging lane imaginable; no sooner had my '61 bus arrived at the end of the grade than it was thrust into traffic moving along at sixty miles an hour. And, of course, most of the other cars on the road expected you to drive like a regular car, and were often infuriated when you couldn't briskly pull into the stream of traffic. Only the big trucks understood, and made allowances. They also knew how susceptible the bus was to being blown off the road when the big rigs passed them at freeway speeds. and usually took care to give them a wide berth.

---

[3] The earlier buses were even worse. When the magazine *Road & Track* tested the 1955 model, it measured a 0-60 mph time of 70 seconds, which was actually almost three times longer than the time it needed to travel a quarter of a mile from a standing start. At that, they had better luck than Britain's *Car Life* magazine, which tried to measure the 0-60 mph time of the 1961 model but couldn't get their bus to reach 60 mph.

Add to that the necessity of shifting (until 1973, buses were bereft of automatic transmissions) and the need to choose, at any of a variety of speeds, the optimum gear for that speed, and you had even more reason to pay attention to what you were doing. The range of speed for each gear was not great, and you exceeded it at your peril, either by lugging the engine below that speed or over-revving above it. Either situation would drastically affect your engine's longevity. So you had to keep one eye focused on the traffic down the road, to prepare for slowdowns and red lights, while your other eye was scanning the rear-view mirrors for traffic behind you (which inevitably would be, in a matter of minutes, traffic around you and then in front of you).

The VW bus's heating system was a joke. The engine powered a blower that forced air over the engine cylinders to keep them cool. That same blower diverted some of that air into compartments that enclosed the exhaust manifolds. The air was then expected to travel the entire length of the car, from the rear to the front, eventually being discharged through vents under the dashboard. At best, it could be expected to raise the temperature of the bus's interior only about twenty degrees Fahrenheit above the temperature outside. Not surprisingly, a brisk aftermarket in separate gasoline-fired heaters sprang up in the less temperate parts of the country.

The Transporter acquired a somewhat undeserved reputation for unreliability, as its engines were never really designed for quick acceleration or freeway speeds in the first place. While most vehicles of that era could achieve about a hundred thousand miles between major engine overhauls, the bus was lucky to reach fifty thousand miles, unless you drove it very conservatively, in which case you might get sixty or seventy thousand miles. And American mechanics, who usually had never seen an air-cooled engine larger than a lawnmower engine before, were unfamiliar with the special requirements of these beasts. For example, there wasn't much oil capacity, and what oil there was took a long time to drain back down into the sump where the dipstick measured the oil level. Add oil to an engine that was idling or had just been switched off, and you were likely to over-fill it, leading to a blown front engine seal and oil leaking

21

all over your clutch and onto the pavement. And if you broke down in an area that didn't have a VW dealership or a knowledgeable service center, you were in serious trouble. Even VW recognized this problem, and made sure that no Beetles or buses were sold in an area unless there were service departments that could repair them, which meant that you were generally OK as long as you stayed near civilization.

Like all VWs, the design was tinkered with over the years, with continually upgraded components like engines, transmissions, and brakes enclosed within a body that stayed pretty much the same from year to year. Unless you were versed in the arcana of VW bodies, such as slightly different turn signal arrangements or larger rear hatch windows, it wasn't easy to determine which model year you were looking at. The first really big change came in 1968, when the split front windshield was replaced with a single curved piece of glass, and the double doors on the side with a single sliding door (available earlier as an option, but now standard equipment). Among other refinements, the new design also featured a slightly more aerodynamic body shape, improved crashworthiness, roll-down windows, a re-designed dashboard and a re-designed rear suspension that got rid of the old swing axles and transfer cases in favor of constant-velocity joints. This body shape survived more or less unchanged until 1980, when the VW Transporter was officially renamed the Vanagon, and again drastically re-designed. This new car was longer, lower, wider, and heavier, and would soon sport a water-cooled engine. There are a lot of people who feel that these vans weren't really buses any more. In the US, they were marketed not as delivery vans but simply as people-carriers and campers, markets where they had no real competition until U.S. carmakers came out with their own versions of the "Microbus" in the nineteen-eighties.

While VW was doing its best to optimize what was essentially the forty-year-old design of a small van, American carmakers re-invented it. Chrysler took the chassis of a front-wheel-drive car, put a van-like body on it with three rows of seating, and called it the Minivan. It was advertised as the next generation of station wagon, a van you could park in your garage and drive like a real car. Almost overnight, the cars became best sellers and spawned copycat designs from nearly every major automaker ... except Volkwagen. It would be almost ten years before VW would come out with its own version of the front-wheel-drive small van, by which time their rivals' lead had become insurmountable.

But the original buses never went away. VW had engineered them to hold up far beyond the lifespan of other vehicles, and hold up they did. While other cars became more technologically advanced, the Transporter remained easy for the shade-tree mechanic to diagnose and repair. The relative simplicity of the VW engine (and the continued availability of that John Muir book) made the VW an attractive choice for the do-it-yourselfer who wanted to keep his or her ride going with a minimum of trouble and money. Which is also why, in south and central America, the bus would continue to be made right up to the beginning of the new century, although it was no longer legal to import them into the United States due to tougher emissions standards that air-cooled engines couldn't satisfy. The drivers of the emerging third world needed a vehicle that could carry great loads over bad roads on a shoestring, and the Transporter was, and still is, the answer for many of them.

Meanwhile, the air-cooled bus has become a quaint oddity on American roads, sure to turn heads, particularly if it's a camper or flatbed truck or some other specialized form of the breed. It may even be a little easier to drive one in traffic now; older drivers remember how sluggish it can be, and newer ones are so taken aback by the rarity of this weird van that they regard it with some caution, or cut it some slack by virtue of its novelty. There's no doubt that I get a lot more stares and questions when I park it now, and more than a few people have taken an extra minute to inspect the interior and reminisce about their own experiences with buses long ago. Of course, those buses of the sixties and seventies represent the same span of time from the present as those old Model T and Model A Fords did to that era, and evoke the same nostalgia that those early models did in the sixties.

VW People

A car as quixotically charming as the VW bus deserves an equally eccentric fan base, and this one has it in spades. I can't explain it, but the VW bus seems to attract more than its usual share of people who want to live their lives their own way, and do what others won't. Maybe it's a holdover from the days when the bus was the unofficial vehicle of the counter-culture. Or maybe it's because the bus fills a niche in the vehicle world that no other vehicle can.

There's no question in my mind that ownership of a bus marks people in distinctive ways that they acknowledge long after they've sold their buses and moved on. I've talked to people who have owned them by the hundreds, always looking for a new bus to restore and put back on the road. On the other end of the spectrum, I've met people who see me get out of my 1971 camper in the supermarket parking lot, and feel the need to tell me about the trips they once took or the bus they once owned. Nine times of of ten, they quickly add that they'll never buy another one, but they still insist that they would not have missed the experience for all the world.

A month doesn't go by when I hear of an adventurous person or family buying a bus and taking it around the country, or around the world, or into areas not frequented by civilization, and blogging every step of their journey or posting their progress on Facebook. I won't name any of them in particular, since their journeys will be over by the time this book goes to print, but there will be others to replace them. The usual scenario is as follows: a young couple finds that their life in a nine-to-five job is unrewarding, and decide to shuck it all and take to the road. Sometimes there's a child, or a dog, who is along for the ride. They travel the entire length or width of their continent, sometimes on the most unimproved roads they can find. Their blogs or Facebook posts have pictures of their bus in front of spectacular scenery – imposing mountains or deserted coastlines – or on the side of lonesome roads. Every picture says "We're here, and you're not."

For another example, there are the people who participate in a unique yearly excursion called the Shasta Snow Trip. Participation is limited to pre-1968 buses, which are usually prized by their owners and never subjected to harsh driving conditions. But not these buses. These buses are rusty and dented, with stripped-down interiors. To look at them, you'd think they were only a step or two away from the crushers. Everything about them screams, "Show me your worst. I've been through it before, and I'm still here." But their high ground clearance and geared-down rear wheels make them remarkably adept at scrambling through what might be charitably described as "unimproved road," and their engines, drivetrains, and brakes are as mechanically perfect as their owners can make them … or at least reliable enough to survive three hundred and fifty miles or so of desolation. They carry spare engines and transmissions, along with the tools to install them. The idea is to make the trip in around fifteen hours, although making it at all without needing a tow or an overhaul is considered to be a success.

The Shasta Snow Trip starts at Willits, California and ends somewhere in the area of Mount Shasta City, but the participants use back country roads, logging trails, or sometimes no roads at all. They encounter mud, streams, and snowdrifts. Their buses are equipped with all-terrain tires and roof racks piled with all the parts and tools they might need to make repairs in the middle of nowhere. They sport extra lights and oversize bumpers. At an auto show at Kelley Park, in San Jose, I saw a bus that had gone off the road and rolled twice. It was severely bent out of shape, with webbing straps holding the doors in place. Why was it at the show? Bragging rights, of course. Nothing else could have conveyed the message "I survived the Shasta Snow Trip" more effectively.

And I have to mention a gentleman who is, as far as I know, the world's only itinerant auto mechanic. His name is Colin Kellogg, and he tours the United States each summer after setting up appointments over the winter with the people who want what he calls "hands-on real-time advice" while they work on their cars. Once the requests are lined up, he works out a circuit, which he calls an "Itinerary," of the country to meet them. He runs all of this through his web site, Itinerant Air-Cooled.

Here's how it works. If you want him to visit you, you make contact with him over the winter and spring. At this time, you generate a "List Of Concerns," order the required parts, and give him a $250.00 deposit (at this writing) to lock in your agreed-upon appointment date, On that date, you'll spend what he describes as a challenging nine-hour day learning how to maintain and repair your air-cooled vehicle and, in Colin's words, "survive the rapid-fire questions of the 'final exam' that yields the invoice, pay the balance of $250.00, then take the next eleven months executing all of the suggestions and recommendations." He has all of the required tools, but expects you to have a set, too, and use it as much as possible. To quote from his web site: "I am a consultant. You are paying for my tutelage. If I pick up a tool, it is to hand it to you." He's earned his living at this for the past fourteen years, and has no plans at present to quit.

I had lunch with him a few years ago, and he filled me in on how he got started in this unusual line of work. In October of 2002, when he was working in the heating and air conditioning field in upstate New York, he joined the nascent air-cooled VW forum called the Samba under the name "Amskeptic", and built a reputation as one of the more knowledgeable people on the forum. Eight months later, he drove across the country to help a fellow member of the Samba rebuild his engine in Los Angeles. "Why not make a business of this?" his friend suggested. Within the year, he decided to take his expertise with air-cooled Volkswagens on the road, having already operated what he called a "mobile BMW Porsche MB VW Whatever business" while attending UCLA in the 1980s.

He set up his own web site in 2006, patterned loosely on the Samba but reflecting his own view on how a forum should work. The Itinerant Air-Cooled web site (IAC) has a special forum for the free expression of political views, which the Samba banned long ago. "We are citizens first, hobbyists second," the IAC site explains. "We invite you to participate using your advanced adult behavior skill set." The political discourse has indeed been well-reasoned and polite for the most part.

But politics constitute only a very small part of the IAC web site. Colin lists the major components for me: "A group of Technical Forums address repair advice, Vehicle Forums provide resources for the specific models, Community Forums offer announcements of club events, shows, and classified ads for cars and parts. At the top of the main page is the growing list of annual Itineraries, each a forum in their own right, with travel stories and photographs of the visits with my clients and some of the gorgeous places in the country I have traveled and camped in. Each Itinerary Forum has the annual 'Results Just In!' post that shows how the business is performing."

Colin put 588,000 miles on the Road Warrior, his beloved 1973 bus, before it was demolished in a head-on collision with another car in 2009 (Colin walked away from that crash). He bought another bus from a fellow member of the forum. This one was a 1978 bus with 34,900 original miles; he made two Itineraries with that car. Next came a 1970 bus, bought from yet another forum member, which made two Itineraries. He recently acquired a 1977 Westfalia camper with an original 42,000 miles to add to the rotation. "With a yearly accumulation of 25,000 miles per itinerary," he says, "I think I can safely run out my clock now ..."

You'll meet a lot more of these people in the following pages, and you'll see a common thread. They have found their own special niche in the Volkswagen bus world. Some of them are evangelists, singing the vehicle's praises. Some spend large chunks of their lives organizing shows and clubs. Some are ace mechanics and machinists, quietly staying in the background and keeping these weird beasts running. They are indispensable in their own way, and the Volkswagen world is the sum of their parts.

Let's get to know them, shall we?

First Encounter

It all began, as Bob Weir sang, when the bus came by and he got on. That bus was Ken Kesey's Further, which Tom Wolfe immortalized in his book *The Electric Kool-Aid Acid Test*. Mine was a green Volkswagen camper that pulled up to our house on Dwight Way in Berkeley, California at ten in the evening. When I got on that bus, the adventure began.

It wasn't the first VW bus I'd ever seen, of course. I grew up in Germany in the fifties and sixties, when Volkswagen buses were commonly used there for delivery vehicles, people-movers, and ambulances. I must have seen a thousand of them around Frankfurt, and they were in no way remarkable. In my teen-age American mindset, I guess I lumped them together with all the other strange little vehicles that I had never seen back in the States: the VW Beetles, the strange three-wheeled Messerschmidts, the Isettas that opened from the front, and the boxy little delivery trucks. They weren't quite real cars, the way the big American Packards and Chevys were. They were more like larger-than-life toys.

When I was eighteen, I went back to the United States to attend college, where I managed to get through three years at the Johns Hopkins University without doing an awful lot of studying. Instead, I found myself busy with running a coffee-house (which included everything from handling its publicity to brewing the coffee), tutoring inner-city kids, doing some draft-counseling, working at a campus radio station, and generally learning about everything except what I was supposed to be studying. My grades plummeted, and I flunked out.

I worked at an electronics wholesaler to earn enough money to fly out to Berkeley, California and live there for a season while looking for a job. This was in 1970, and jobs were scarce, particularly for college drop-outs with no real work experience. In May, my father called to tell me that I'd gotten an offer from the Baltimore City Health Department to be what they called a "Health Educator Aide" on the rat eradication program that was going into full swing at that time. If I could get to Baltimore by mid-June, I had the job. So I photocopied about a dozen "ride wanted" posters – the kind with the tear-off tags at the bottom – and posted them on Telegraph Avenue and in various hang-outs on the University of California campus. And that's how I first got on intimate terms with the Volkswagen bus.

On the evening of June 4, 1970, I was eating supper at a church-sponsored soup kitchen when I was called to the phone. My brother's girlfriend was on the line; she told me that some people from Palo Alto had seen my ad and were on their way to pick me up. I was down to the $85 I had saved for Greyhound bus fare in case I couldn't get a ride, and had been left in the lurch twice before by rides that didn't materialize. I could no longer afford the seventy-cent "Gross-burgers" and Cokes I'd been subsisting on, and was saving my stash for the Big Trip. This ride was the last gamble I intended to take because time was running out on the Baltimore opportunity. So I went home to pack and wait.

At 10:00 p.m., a dark green VW camper pulled up to the driveway and bleeped. I shook a few hands, caught a glimpse of some faces, roped my luggage to the rack on the top of the bus, and in two minutes flat we were on the road.

My traveling companions turned out to be four people of my approximate age. There was Ed DuBose, big and black; his wife Shelley, very white and blond and small; Joel, an itinerant musician; and another person whose name I've forgotten. There was also a black puppy named Striker, after the student strike at Ed's college.

The trip across the country took eight days. I did more than my share of the driving, since I knew how to drive a stick shift. My first turn at the wheel was taking the bus downhill from Donner Pass to Reno, which we hit at about four in the morning. In those days, the interstate stopped at the edge of town, where it became a boulevard that swept us past the Happy Bells Wedding Chapel and countless bars and casinos, all garishly lit. We didn't stop until sunrise, when we refueled and ate breakfast in Lovelock.

29

I slept for a while, and then took another turn at the wheel as we drove into Utah. We hit a hellacious rain-storm as we drove by the Salt Flats – high headwinds, slashes of rain that overpowered our windshield wipers, and tumbleweeds coming up out of nowhere and crashing into the front of the bus as we sped past a landscape of white and greenish-gray.

Our interracial couple drew a lot of stares, most of them unfriendly. In Utah, we encountered two police roadblocks, where we were rousted out of the bus with shotguns. The cops at the second roadblock told us they were looking for two robbers, and they thought Joel might have been the one with the beard. The other robber was thought to be a Chicano. Nobody looked like a Chicano. They let us go.

That bus was a split-window camper, probably an early sixties model. Its engine was most likely the 1200 cc engine putting out forty horsepower. With the load it was carrying, Ed decided to treat it to a set of heavy-duty shocks, which he installed while we camped at a truck stop in Salt Lake City.

The bus went through Colorado doing 15 mph up the hills and 30 downhill, but it was reliable and gave us no trouble. Neither did the cops, for the most part, although there were a few uncomfortable encounters in Colorado and Kansas, where interracial couples driving VW buses were still a novelty, and campground owners found it more convenient to call the cops rather than put us up. But there were good cops, too, giving us directions and not writing us up for a broken headlight.

But our luck ran out in Kansas. At some point, the oil filler cap was removed from its pipe and not replaced. Ed suspected sabotage, presumably by some gas station attendant, but it might have been Ed himself forgetting to replace the cap when he topped up the oil, as I myself have come close to doing once in a while. At any rate, the engine started singing its death song about a hundred miles farther down the road. I'd been asleep in the back, and can't remember whether it was that death song or Ed's spate of profanity that awakened me. We opened the engine compartment. The crankcase was dry, oil had spewed all around the engine compartment, and we were in deep trouble. We threw our last can of oil into the engine and proceeded painfully down the road. We somehow got as far as Columbia, which was a college town; we had hoped for a warmer welcome there than our busful of hippies had received elsewhere along the way. The bus made it to the college's residential area where it stopped at the first house and died, probably a victim of oil-starved bearings seizing up.

By incredible chance, the house was occupied by a Tanzanian researcher named Tumaini Mcharo, his American wife, and their children. It was his wife who answered our knock, listened to our story, and called her husband. Suddenly, we had the best possible friends in that town.

Mr. Mcharo turned out to be more than that. He made us his personal guests, and we pushed our bus onto his lawn to keep it from being towed by the campus police. He loaned Ed his car, saying that he preferred to walk the mile to his office anyway. He and his wife kept us fed, washed, and entertained. I still remember his smile when we told him that after all the Christian Americans we had encountered in Missouri, only he – a non-Christian foreigner – had shown us the slightest compassion. He replied that he believed we were all brothers, and that we must help each other because that is what brothers do.

When Ed removed the engine from the bus the next morning, he found that the trouble was too serious to attempt repairs and started to look around for another engine. We located a wrecked VW bus with a fairly decent 1500 cc engine in it, and arranged for a local garage to transplant that engine into our bus. Shelley wired home for $300 to pay for it all, and in two days we were on the road again. The new engine started over-heating once we were back in mountain country, so we would stop at the rest stops and open the hood to let the night air cool the engine off while we walked the dog.

In Harrisburg, Pennsylvania, I parted company with the expedition and caught a Trailways bus just leaving for Washington, D.C. By that time, I had already made the acquaintance of a book called *How to Keep Your Volkwagen Alive: A Manual of Step by Step Procedures for the Compleat Idiot*, which had been of valuable use during our engine mishap, and which was pretty much the only reading material I had other than

31

Frank Herbert's *Dune* books. A notion had formed in my mind that a VW bus wouldn't be a bad sort of car to own, and that this book would help me keep it on the road. I didn't know it then, but a seed had been planted that would be in flower the very next year.

The Idiot Book

Along with the luggage, sleeping bags, and maps in that bus, there was a book with a most curious title: *How to Keep Your Volkswagen Alive: A Manual for the Compleat Idiot.* It was written and self-published in 1969 by John Muir, and purported to be a shop manual for VW repair that anybody could use and understand, even those with a complete ignorance of auto mechanics. And in large measure, it was just that.

I had never seen such a book before. It was written from the standpoint of a witty mechanic who was sitting right next to you as you were doing each procedure, pointing out the things you were supposed to be seeing and describing how to perform the necessary steps. It cheerfully described which procedures were important and required immediate attention, and which procedures were not as important and could wait until you, the poor starving hippie, could scrape together the bread. And he told you what sort of jury-rigged repairs you could get away with until that day arrived. This approach dictated what at first glance seemed a certain whimsy in its layout and chapter sequence; the chapter on tune-ups, which should have been in the front of the book, was buried in the middle.

But once you realized that Muir had prioritized all the procedures that you needed to get going again after some catastrophic failure ("Car Won't Start," "Red Light On," "Volkswagen Won't Stop"), and then brought in the more routine maintenance later, the sequence started to make sense, after a fashion. The book was adorned with copious line illustrations by Peter Aschwanden, a talented cartoonist who captured perfectly both the necessary detail required to understand the procedure and the humor and wit of Muir's write-ups.

The book was a radical change from the usual array of technical manuals, but the concept wasn't exactly new. Muir may have taken the idea from Will Eisner, the artist and writer who is widely regarded as the man who put the modern graphic novel on the literary map. While serving with the army during

World War II, Eisner put out a series of preventive maintenance manuals for the military. *Army Motors* combined cartoons with written essays, all done in a lighthearted style while impressing upon the soldier the importance of preventive maintenance. Characters such as the hapless soldiers Joe Dope and Sergeant Half-Mast introduced the soldiers to the art of keeping their equipment war-worthy. The magazine was a success, and stayed in publication throughout the war. Revived in the 1950s as P★S, and with Eisner on its staff, it ran until 1971. To soothe the fears of the Army brass, Eisner took pains to point out that the magazine was never intended to replace the dry, hard-to-read operating manuals that accompanied military equipment but existed only to supplement them, giving soldiers the basic information in an entertaining style.

Muir wrote the first edition of *How to Keep Your Volkswagen Alive* for those who had the original VW bugs and buses, with the original "upright" engine configuration used by Ferdinand Porsche. There wasn't much difference then between the bug engine and the bus engine, and the same repair procedures would work for either one. Muir himself was a fan of the bus, in which he used to travel around the American Southwest and often into Mexico. He scorned the freeways, preferring the dirt roads and occasionally leaving them for places where there were no roads at all. The bus interested him, he said, because of its high ground clearance, rugged construction, and low gearing. As I've mentioned, its design harked back to the *Kübelwagen*, whose air-cooled engine and gear-reduction boxes sitting over the rear axle made it a surprisingly adept scrambler.

John was trained as an engineer and worked for Lockheed before he dropped out, and he appreciated the VW for the marvel of engineering that it was. It was full of elegant solutions to common automotive problems of power and weight, and would often take a counter-intuitive approach to those problems. For an engineer, this was catnip, and it didn't take a reader long to discover that John Muir was seriously in love with the car and what it could do. There were places in the book where he became positively rhapsodic about it and, the more you read the book, the more that attitude rubbed off on you.

34

The Idiot Book is still in print, a remarkable feat for a technical manual first published nearly fifty years ago. It has sold well over a million copies and is in its nineteenth edition. It has outlived both Muir, who died in 1977, and Aschwanden, who died in 2005. Even though it's been thirty years since VW has imported an air-cooled vehicle into the United States, it continues to sell steadily. It has been heavily revised numerous times to reflect design changes throughout the years and revisions in the procedures made possible from the feedback of the thousands and thousands of people who have used the book. It can be found in the library of nearly everybody who has one of the old air-cooled Volksies, and not uncommonly in the car itself, next to the tool-box. Find a hundred people who have worked on their own Volkswagens, and I'll bet that ninety-nine of them have used the Idiot Book.

My wife's hairdresser sold her bus a few years back, but kept a lot of spare parts and some books in her garage. When she learned that I had recently bought a VW bus, she gave my wife the parts and the books. Among the latter was, of course, the Idiot Book, the 1976 edition, in the classic condition of most of these books, with the front cover fallen off and stains on every other page from grease, oil, and God only knows what other fluids that Leanne's bus had excreted over the years.

I've owned maybe a half a dozen copies of the thing, starting with the 1971 edition, which I used to overhaul the engine on my first bus. Over the years, I replaced it with later editions because I used the book until it fell apart into grease-stained tatters, or because I wanted to take advantage of the continual revisions as they became available.

A lot of people have called this book the indispensable reference for VW owners, and I agree with them. I also agree with those who point out its shortcomings. Muir quoted a friend of his, on a review of another VW book, as saying "I agree one hundred percent with ninety percent of what he says." That could also apply to my own feelings about Muir's book.

As a technical manual, it mostly consists of solid information — solid enough, anyway, to get you back on the road so you can find somebody to show you how to do it the right way. I've always advised a prospective repairer to buy both this book and another manual (my favorite was the green *Volkswagen Official Service Manual*, also called the "Bentley" after its current publisher), read the Muir write-up first to get a general idea of what to do, and then compare it to the other manual, note the differences, and ask somebody why the differences are there. Usually it's because Muir assumes you're making do with a minimum of tools, or are too cash-strapped to make a proper fix.

Occasionally, you'd find that the directions wouldn't describe your particular model, because you had a different set-up than the ones he was familiar with. And there are many mechanics who take issue, sometimes forcefully, with Muir's opinions of how certain repairs were to be performed. Lastly, his advice was often based on his experiences with the earlier of models of Volkswagens, but often contradicted the recommendations that the company made for the service of its later models. For example, he loved the Bosch 009 mechanical-advance distributor, which worked well with earlier carburetors but wasn't very well suited to the more complex carburetors VW began to use in the 1970s, when emission standards became tougher.

But to simply compare this book with other technical manuals would be to ignore its most important, which is its ability to empower you. It presumes that the reader has no technical aptitude and starts you gently down the road to proficiency and self-confidence. (It's a safe bet that more mechanics have been inspired by this book than any other technical manual ever written.) Not only that, but once you have discovered that you can indeed perform a repair competently, you get a sneaking suspicion that there are other things you can do if you apply the same confidence, common sense, and ingenuity that John taught you about. I doubt if I would have had the courage to time a sewing machine, install a hard drive, or build a guitar if John hadn't shown me that I had the potential to do these things if I trusted myself and paid attention to the process.

Nowadays, of course, there are bookshelves full of books, on nearly every conceivable subject, that are oriented toward the

"Dummy" or the "Idiot" (usually referred to as such in the title). Without exception, their authors treat the reader as an intelligent but technically uneducated person who needs a little cheering up, a little hard information, and a lot of reassurance. All these authors owe a great debt to John Muir, whether they realize it or not, because John was among the first to show them the way.[4]

When the book came out in 1969, a sea change was underway in how people viewed technology. It was the same era when the mainframe computer was giving way to smaller computers that allowed people to write their own code instead of accepting the IBM or Honeywell standard, a story brilliantly told in Steve Levy's book *Hackers*. This new attitude toward technology permeated an entire subculture and spawned a host of self-help publications, of which the *Mother Earth News* was the most successful over the long run, with the arguable exception of the Idiot Book itself.

One of 1969's top-selling books was *The Whole Earth Catalog*. First published in 1968, it urged people to return to simplest level of technology — the windmill, the blacksmith's forge, the table-top flour mill — that would do the job for them. The burning question was: who is going to control your life, you or your technology? Will you be technology's master, or its slave?

Now, Muir was no Luddite. He had no grudge against Volkswagen and its army of dealers, garages and mechanics, and he was quick to refer you to them when the repair called for the specialized skills and tools they had. But he felt deeply that when you start to rely on others to do what you can do yourself, you start losing control of your situation. If you adjust your VW's

---

[4] Or almost first. I've mentioned Will Eisner's preventive maintenance publications. And I remember a couple of cookbooks that my mother owned, put out around World War Two by the "Mystery Chef," that applied the same technique to the art of cooking. In the book, he pointed out that water boils at 212° Fahrenheit whether you're a professional chef or somebody cooking an egg for the first time. If you know how to boil water and use a clock, he claimed, you can boil that egg as well as the head chef at the Waldorf. The Mystery Chef, one of the first media chefs (he had a radio show on NBC in the 1930s), was eventually revealed to be John MacPherson; his books were popular from the thirties to the sixties, but are sadly long out of print.

valves yourself every three thousand miles, you know that it was done right, and on schedule, and without shortcuts. If you drain the oil and wash the oil screen yourself, you get information on the engine's health that you never would have gotten otherwise. If you really listen to your engine, you'll hear how the noise changes when something goes wonky, and you might even know what's wrong. Levy called this attitude the "Hands-On Imperative," the urge that impelled people to write code of their own rather than relying on other programmers to write it, to build computers of their own rather than using the hulking giants of science and commerce, and plant gardens rather than buying their veggies at the supermarket. You were in control, not the machine.

Ferdinand Porsche, the designer of the Volkswagen Beetle (and also the godfather of the engine that was to power both the bug and the bus) was no stranger to the Hands-On Imperative. There's an often retold story of how a malfunctioning limousine was brought to the shop at Diamler, where Porsche was employed as a designer during the Roaring Twenties. As the technicians there, all dressed in their spotless white smocks, discussed what might be causing the trouble, only Porsche made the effort to borrow a set of greasy overalls from a mechanic, crawl under the car, and investigate the problem for himself. He found the defect and, as he doffed the overalls, the technicians asked him what it was. "Look for yourselves," Porsche snapped as he strode away.

The Idiot Book has survived because of its idiosyncrasies, not in spite of them. John writes that "You must do this work with love or you will fail. You don't have to think, but you must love." He's telling you something important about life here, and about the relationship we have to our possessions and to our work. Forty years later, these are still wise words, and to find them in an automotive manual is astonishing. Robert Pirsig's *Zen and the Art of Motorcycle Maintenance* tried to apply philosophical principles to machine repair, but he failed because he wasn't much of a mechanic and tried to gauge a mechanic's skill according to his own expectations of what a mechanic's mind-set should be. John knew better. He knew, and taught, that you achieve oneness with the machine by applying mind, heart, and hands together, and by listening to the machine as it tries to tell you what needs to be done. If there's ever been another technical book like that, I haven't heard of it. And if there is, I'll wager that the author has read the Idiot Book.

Pink Bus

I got the job with the Baltimore City Health Department and began working for them in June of 1970. My father had given me an Oldsmobile F-85 to get around in, but that car died during the winter and I couldn't afford to fix it, so I gave it to a mechanic friend of mine to sell for me and started taking the city bus to work. I also went back to school, studying at Antioch College's Baltimore branch, where I met some other students who planned to establish a weekly independent newspaper. The *Baltimore Independent* was started as an exercise in community organization and was funded by a small grant from a local college, which was giving us academic credit for our activity. Tom, Gail, and I were determined not to make it look like the "underground" papers so prevalent in that era, so we kept the format conservative and sober. Maybe a little too sober, in fact— it failed after three or four issues, but we kept the company afloat for another couple of years, publishing short-run newsletters and promotional materials for other businesses.

We set up offices on 12 W. 25th Street, just west of Charles Street. That building doesn't exist any more; when I visited the area in 2005, I found a new CVS Pharmacy on that corner. If you wanted to know what the old building looked like, you need to travel one block farther west, where identical buildings still stand. One of those buildings housed the offices of *Folk Forum*, a folk-music magazine published by Bob Cadwallader.

I would contribute an occasional article or cartoon to *Folk Forum* magazine, and did a little free-lance artwork for Bob. He had an assistant named Margie Weigel, whom I would often see answering the phones or typesetting the magazine when I stopped by. Margie was a slender woman with long brown hair and elfin features who would sometimes play one of the guitars that always seemed to be around the office. Within a few months, she would be my girlfriend. Two years later, she would be my wife.

Bob figures in this narrative because he owned one of those early VW buses. It was the kind called the "23-window" because it had not only the fifteen windows that came standard with that line of bus, but an additional four windows along each side of the roof. It also had a sliding roof, which came in handy when Bob, Margie and I went shopping for a Christmas tree that year. He opened the roof, and the tree projected from the top of the van. At the time, I was fresh from my experience with Ed's bus, and it seemed natural to think that that a bus could be in my future, too.

Margie and I had been living together for a while in unwedded bliss when we decided that the time had come to buy a car. She wanted a bus like Bob's, and I didn't complain. After all, I had read enough of John Muir's Idiot Book to feel confident about fixing anything on it that broke, so we started looking in the papers.

One day, I arrived home from my job at the Health Department to find Margie standing at the door with the newspaper. She had found a bus, she said. It was a 1961 bus in "good running condition" and cost $700. The odometer read twenty-five thousand, which meant nothing really ... it couldn't register more than 99,999 miles before resetting to zero, and an eleven-year-old bus would be expected to have at least 125,000 miles on it. For all I know, it could have been 225,000 miles.

We borrowed a car and went out to take a look at it. It turned out to be a fifteen-window bus, one notch up in grade from the thirteen-window configuration (the rear quarter-panels of the bus were glazed rather than metal). It had been originally painted in what VW called "sealing-wax red," which was a sort of coral or flamingo red, but the paint had faded over ten years to a sort of pastel pink. The bus was missing its middle seat, but in addition to the rear bench seat, we also got a folding piece of plywood covered with foam and carpeting which could be used as a bed when we took the rear seat out.

One of its previous owners had put curtains in every window behind the driver's compartment. Since it was a '61, it had no gas gauge; instead, it had a one-gallon reserve tank that you had to remember to keep filled. We started it up and the engine

41

seemed strong. The owner told us that it was actually a 1300 Bug engine rather than the stock 1200 engine, giving a 25% boost in horsepower. Using the Idiot Book I'd just bought, we checked out all the systems and found nothing we couldn't repair except the swing lever bushing, which had corroded to the point where considerable strength was necessary to turn the steering wheel. When I pointed this out to the owner, he dropped the price to $650, which I paid in cash. With Margie following in the borrowed car, I drove the thing back home. Before the week was out, we had the steering bushing replaced at the VW dealership and had given the bus a complete tune-up and oil change.

That fall, disaster struck the Pink Bus. I had left it parked in front of our apartment on Maryland Avenue, one of the major south-bound arteries in the city, where parking was banned during the morning commute hours. I was sick with the flu at the time, and had overslept. By the time I got to the street, the bus had already been towed away.

That wouldn't have been so bad, except that the tow truck towed it just the way it towed every other car, by lifting the front end and leaving the rear wheels on the ground. However, the bus had been left in gear, and the driver had neglected to shift the bus into neutral. An automatic-transmission car, shifted into "park" would probably not have rolled at all, but our bus did, and the four-mile tow to the impound lot trashed the heads of the engine completely. When I started the engine, it groaned horribly and refused to go more than a couple of miles an hour. The sound was so alarming that I drove for only a few blocks before I lost heart, parked the car where it wouldn't be towed again, and took the city bus home.

Margie called a friend of hers. He hooked the bus to his truck and we towed it to a little private garage just north of the city line. The garage belonged to John Deford, a printer who had a shop just a half a block from our offices at the *Independent*. His specialty was printing books with limited press runs, such as law books and genealogical records. Whenever our company had a job that required a lot of collating and stapling, John would run it through a contraption that used a bewildering network of conveyor belts and vacuum tubes to move the sheets of paper where they needed to be. That machine was a marvel when it was working properly, but it required constant attention and induced many colorful turns of phrase from John when it misbehaved.

As I recuperated from the flu, I read and re-read John Muir's procedure on rebuilding the engine. I already had most of the tools, and was able to borrow a few more from John's son, who had been an auto mechanic. It was late in the fall, and by the time I got home from work, had a quick dinner, and rode the city bus up to John's house, it was already dark. I would work for a couple of hours in the freezing cold, washing parts in gasoline by the light of a single electric bulb.

After a few nights of this, John took pity on me and invited me into the house and gave me shots of whiskey to fortify me against the cold. We'd talk in his kitchen for fifteen minutes while the whiskey took effect, and back into the cold I would go for another hour. John was a marvelous raconteur, extraordinarily well-read, and could converse at length on any subject, particularly politics. He and I both subscribed to the *New Yorker* magazine, and would discuss each week's issue in detail. Like my father, he had been in the Army Air Forces; John flew cargo planes, while my father did maintenance on the gun turrets of bombers.

Working nights and weekends in this fashion for three weeks, I was able to rebuild the engine and re-install it. John's son happened to be visiting when I made the final electrical connections and started it up. He said that everything sounded just fine to him. We checked the compression and timing, and the engine passed with flying colors. I drove home with a sense of accomplishment I'd never experienced before.

Margie was the bus's principal driver, since she needed it to get to school while it was more convenient for me to take public transit to work. I would occasionally use the Pink Bus for the health inspections I performed during the summers in lieu of my usual duties as a "health educator," which consisted of teaching kids in the public schools the basics of public sanitation. It proved much easier to maneuver in the narrow alleys than the

43

Ford Econolines that the city provided for us, and there were few alleyways in downtown Baltimore that I didn't drive through to avoid the street traffic. It also served as a cargo van to move the household good of several friends, as all VW buses are obliged to do at some point. The most notable of these missions happened when a geologist friend needed someone to move her rock collection across town. The load of rocks turned out to weigh over a ton, and we moved them all in one trip, overloading the poor bus by several hundred pounds. The progress was excruciatingly slow, as we were afraid to tax the brakes or the suspension system with any unnecessary stresses, but we made the trip without ill effects.

When, in the course of our education efforts at the health department, we needed a vehicle to transport exhibits, we used the bus. Festooned with posters, it served as an eye-catching display board, attracting more attention than the Econolines could. Since my hair was shoulder-length at the time, it made perfect sense that I would be driving a "hippie bus" around town. Charlie, one of

Pink Bus at work.

my associates, was a part-time male model who, wearing a daishiki and sporting an Afro, appeared as "Brother Bo" on countless billboards for a local brewery; Tony was an aspiring rhythm-and-blues singer who punctuated his lectures with song. Together, we made a distinctive team that kids would actually pay some attention to. (Charlie would eventually become president of a college, while Tony would later make his reputation as one of the country's best Sammy Davis impersonators. I was in more august company than I knew.)

The Pink Bus was also occasionally used as a camper. My teen-age sister was living with us at the time, and she and I took the bus to Shenandoah National Park, on Skyline Drive in Virginia. We arrived at our campsite to find it strewn with pieces of Styrofoam, and the people in the adjacent campsite told us that they had just been visited by a black bear that demolished their ice chest in search of food. My sister and I resolved to keep our food, and ourselves, in the bus, although we contrived a sort of "bear alarm" using a tin pan, a twig, and a marshmallow. My sister kept a vigil, but the alarm never went off.

Margie and I shared a rowhouse for a year in Charles Village, near the Johns Hopkins University with Tom and Gail, my old friends from the *Baltimore Independent*, who had moved back from southern Virginia. At the end of that year, we got married and moved north to a little house in Towson for a year. (That little house doesn't exist any more, either.) We continued to drive the Pink Bus back and forth to Virginia to visit my parents, and occasionally took trips to upstate New York, the Shenandoah Valley, and Ocean City on Maryland's eastern shore.

During the gas crunch of the early seventies, when gas stations would close after selling their allotment of fuel, Margie and I calculated that if we left Towson with a full tank we could just barely make the round trip to my parents' house in Falls Church, Virginia without having to risk stopping along the way to refuel. In the winter, the bus's lack of heat made the trip an uncomfortable one, and I remember one Christmas visit where we sang carols at the top of our lungs to take our mind off the chill.

Margie, whose taste in cars ran to small, sporty cars, came to dislike the bus, and we sold it in the spring of 1975 to buy another car she wanted, a Renault R-16 owned by Don Clarke, who was rooming with us at the time. Long before I met Margie, she and Don had driven to the West Coast and back in the Renault, towing a small camper-trailer. I think she was looking for a way to recapture her teen-age years. The suspicion became stronger that fall when she told me that she wanted a divorce so she could pick up where she had left off all those years ago, and once again be the free spirit he had been in her teens.

The previous summer, we had bought another bus as a second car for me. This one was a red 1970 bus, outfitted as a stock "station wagon" model. Bought for $1500, it was mechanically sound but suffered from some rusting in the rocker panels above the floor pan. (The rust turned out to be far more

45

extensive than I first thought, and doomed the car to a premature death, but not before I had put another hundred thousand miles on it.) I took the bus on a shake-down cruise up to New Hampshire, where I visited a cousin, and to Big Moose Lake in the Adirondacks of upstate New York, where I helped my uncle put a roof on his neighbor's cabin. This bus was far more roadworthy than the Pink Bus. It got better mileage and had a bigger gas tank, resulting in greater range between fill-ups, and had the power to keep up with traffic on the interstates, even up shallow grades, a feat the Pink Bus could never manage.

When Margie and I split up, she took the Renault and I took the bus. I had just changed careers that fall, quitting the health department to work for a small hang glider factory and school in nearby Libertyville. That was Don's fault, too. He was working weekends as an instructor for the school, and he'd talked me into taking a few lessons. It wasn't long before I became hooked. Hang gliding as an industry was in its infancy at the time, and it was like watching an entire kind of aviation growing up before my eyes. "This is what it must have been like working for the Wright brothers!" I thought. The owner of the hang-gliding school offered me a job building and repairing his gliders for a reasonable salary and free lessons.

In the space of a couple of months, my life had turned completely upside down. When the fall of 1975 started I was a civil servant with a wife and an unsatisfying job. When it ended, I was single, barely employed, and living by myself in a small apartment in a converted farm-house in Sykesville, Maryland. The only constants I had in my life were some friends whose friendship had survived the divorce, and the new bus. Before five years were out, I and that 1970 bus would be on the other side of the continent, with almost nothing left of my former life.

Blunder Bus

My first major experience with the 1970 bus was not auspicious. A few months after I bought it, it caught fire.

I was driving down the Jones Falls Expressway north of Baltimore when I suddenly lost power. I pulled over to the side of the road. A pungent odor was filling the air; I looked into the back of the bus, and saw smoke. Not good.

I got out. Smoke was pouring out of the air intake vents. I popped the rear engine hatch, and more smoke came out. My puny three-pound fire extinguisher had no effect, except perhaps to slow the progress of the fire a little. Just then, a Maryland State Police prowler was passing in the opposite direction. He stopped and got on the bullhorn.

"IS THAT CAR ON FIRE?"

I nodded energetically. The cops traversed the median strip and pulled up to a cautious distance behind the bus, and hit their flashers. Within minutes, a fire truck pulled up next to the blazing bus. The firemen unlimbered their high-pressure hose and directed a ten-second blast of water into the engine compartment. The push was so strong that the bus skidded forward, even though I had put the parking brake on and left it in first gear. I had always been told never to put water on a gasoline fire, because that would spread the fire, but that gush of water did the trick, for sure. I later realized that the water almost instantly cooled everything down to below the ignition point; there was not enough heat left to sustain the fire.

Eventually the fire truck left, leaving me and the cops looking into what was left of the engine compartment. The engine itself was barely recognizable. All that remained of the carburetor was a little puddle of aluminum resting on the steel pulley shroud. The battery had melted. All the wiring in the engine compartment had crisped, along with most of the paint inside and around the engine compartment. To my great relief, the tires survived unscathed, and the fire never penetrated to the passenger compartment itself. The bus was severely maimed, but not totaled. It would even roll.

The cops told me that I couldn't get a ride in their car unless I was arrested, but they could have headquarters phone somebody to pick me up and rescue me. An hour later, Don Clarke came by with his Japanese pickup truck, and we towed the bus to the hang glider shop where I had just been employed.

Bob Martin, the proprietor of the shop, hadn't expect to fit in an engine overhaul into the rest of the glider manufacturing and repair that was his business, but he took it all in good grace. The ruined bus was parked outside, anyway, and didn't take up any shop space. He even loaned me his car so I could go shopping for another engine.

I found one in East Baltimore. It had just come out of a 1971 bus that somebody had front-ended. The bus was a loss, crumpled like an accordian from the front bumper to the front wheels, but everything behind the driver's seat appeared to be undamaged. I took out the engine, the generator, the battery, and as much of the wiring harnesses as I could scavenge. The total bill came to about five hundred dollars, if I remember correctly, plus all the wiring and terminals I would need to splice the wiring harnesses into what was left of my bus's original wiring.

My first job, of course, was to remove as much of the burnt paint as possible and cover the bare metal with brown primer, inside and out. That was the hardest part of the job, and the dirtiest. Then came the tedious job of matching each wire in each harness to its corresponding wire on the chassis, grafting extensions where necessary to replace the burned sections between the scavenged harness and the original wire.

After that, the engine installation itself was surprisingly painless. The 1970 and 1971 engines were virtually identical; the only real difference was that the newer engine had a vacuum port in the intake manifold to accommodate the power brakes that Volkswagen had introduced that year. I plugged the port, and the engine went in without a hitch. I was back on the road within a few days and, except for the weird paint job and an odor of burning plastic and rubber that never really did go away, it bore no traces of its ordeal.

When I had used this bus as a camper the previous summer, I re-used the plywood sleeping platform we had in the Pink Bus. But this wasn't the ideal solution for somebody who was planning to do a lot of camping in the future (and who would end up doing a lot more of it than he had ever dreamed). I decided I wanted a real camper-bus, with all the trimmings. I had planned to trade the Blunder Bus in on one, but the fire disaster had sucked up a good chunk of the thousand dollars that I would need to make the upgrade, and also had reduced the trade-in value of the bus to practically nothing. So that plan was shot.

But I got my camper anyway. Here's how it happened.

Not having money to buy something didn't keep me from looking, and eventually I found a camper in the paper selling for three hundred dollars. At that price, there had to be something wrong with it. But I went out to look at it anyway.

It turned out to be a 1964 VW Westfalia camper rusting peacefully to death out in a Maryland cornfield. The body was rusted beyond recovery, with hardly any floor left and huge holes on nearly every body panel. The salted roads of winter had not been kind to this bus. The owner said that it still ran when he last started it, but that the transmission wouldn't shift out of first gear. The engine sounded like it was firing on only three cylinders, and the lights didn't work.

But the camper bits were almost pristine. It had the bench seat that converted into a bed, a pop-top that expanded the headroom by two feet, an ice-box, numerous tables that folded away, and a water tank with a little faucet you could pump to get the water out. Plus lots of cabinets.

Well, I already had a bus. Now I could get the camper innards, and combine them into a camper. Nowadays, it would be considered sacrilegious to tear apart a gen-u-wine '64 Westfalia camper, except to provide parts for another gen-u-wine Westfalia camper, but this one was clearly doomed.

I bought the camper, paid the hippie-turned-corn-farmer, and drove it very slowly and painfully down to the People's Garage, a sort of workshop-cum-commune in the Charles Village area of Baltimore. There I dismantled it, taking all the camper bits from the pop-top down to the last cabinet. I donated the rest of the bus to the commune, who would be free to take whatever parts they deemed worth taking and sell the rest for scrap.

Back home, I fitted the pieces onto and into my bus. Since the body shapes of the '64 and '70 buses were slightly different, a certain amount of trimming and fitting was necessary, but it all worked in the end. I now had what bus mavens call a "Frankenwestie" composed of odd bits of various buses and campers. I didn't care. It was a perfectly serviceable camper.

Since there was a cabinet that went where the spare tire well went, I moved the spare to a bracket I installed on the front of the bus. This sort of bracket is not well thought of by the people who do bodywork, since it tends to distort the front metal unless it is properly installed (and practically none of them are). But I never had any trouble with it and, as it turned out, a little warpage of the nose would turn out to be the least of my worries concerning that particular bus's bodywork.

I also found out how steady the ride of the bus was. When installing the pop-top, I traced out the part of the roof that needed to be removed with a felt marker. After the roof was cut out and the pop-top was installed, I went on a flying trip to West Virginia, where the bus was used to pick up gliders from a recently harvested cornfield that had been pressed into service as a landing area. There was no road handy for the last quarter-mile or so, so I got a taste of how the bus handled off the road as it bounced across the furrows. We broke down the gliders and loaded them on to the bus's roof racks. As I loaded the first one, I noticed something laying in the rain gutter ... the felt marker, still there after that bone-jarring drive.

I drove down to Florida that Christmas to see my parents, who had retired to a new community in Port Richey. I remember taking the bus to a garage there for a lube job. By and by, the garage man came over and said, "Your bus has no heat."

"Well, it's a bus," I replied. "The heat's not very good at best."

"No," he said. "Your bus has *no* heat." And he took me back to the service bay, where the bus was on a lift, and showed me why. Somewhere on the journey south, the entire pipe that

50

transferred hot air from the heat-exchanger boxes to the front of the car had fallen off. So my next stop was a home-improvement center, where I bought ten feet of four-inch PVC pipe and somehow installed it in place of the missing pipe.

While I was at it, I also dug out the rust underneath the rocker panels. Dad showed me how quick body repairs were done when he was young; you taped over the holes with a fabric-based tape like duct tape, painted over the tape, and hoped that the patch would survive until you got enough money together to fix it right. In this case, the patch lasted for the rest of the life of the bus, which turned out to be about five years. We also pop-riveted steel flashing onto the rusted-out areas of the sliding door's roller track.

In 1976, Bob Martin got the idea that the Deep Creek Lake area of western Maryland would be the perfect place to establish a branch of his hang gliding school. He spoke glowingly of the resorts and the tourism in that area during the summer, and envisioned the sort of "take the tourists in and give them hang glider rides" business concept that had worked so well for Kitty Hawk Kites on the Outer Banks of North Carolina. The idea was to rebuild an old building (formerly a skeet-shooting shop) on the ground of the Wisp ski area, open a hang glider school and pro shop, and rake in the money. We would live at a campground on the lake, where I could live in my bus and he and his family would live in a little tent-trailer.

Well, we did live at the campground all summer, and we started to rebuild the shed, but that was as far as the dream got. The tourists didn't materialize. The economy was bad, Bob explained. Next year would be better. Next year would work, for sure.

I found out something about the bus, though. It was comfortable enough to live in for extended periods of time. The only things it really lacked were a toilet and a shower, and as long as those could be provided at the campground and the ski area, it was not difficult for a young man without family or connections to adapt to that life-style. My old friends were shaking their heads, wondering what had become of that civil servant who liked sleeping in proper beds and cooking proper

51

meals; a few wondered if my divorce hadn't forced me off some mental cliff into ruin. Their worries were groundless; the almost monastic existence was just what I needed to regain my bearings.

I found that, for the first time in my life, I had less living space than I ever thought I needed, and adjustments had to be made. It was a lot like living in a tipi, or on a boat. The cardinal rule of living in a small space is the same cardinal rule of the universe itself: Thou Shalt Not Waste.

Waste meant more than simply using two paper towels where one would do, or tossing out paper bags and newspapers which would turn out to be necessary to get the fire started. It meant applying the concept of economy to the living space itself. Excluding the driver's compartment, the bus provided a living space eleven feet by five feet by four and a half feet, or just under two hundred fifty cubic feet into which to put kitchen, bed, luggage, library, pantry, garage, and closet.

Crises developed. Can one can of peaches be stored? Can two? What was the minimum amount of clothing I need for this season? I learned to play a penny-whistle ... less space than a guitar occupies.

By heating an extra pint of water with my evening tea and storing it overnight in a Thermos bottle, I had enough hot water to reconstitute some dried potatoes for breakfast without having to wait for the Coleman stove to heat up the morning's coffee water. The stove was burning for a shorter time, saving fuel (which also had to be stored).

I bought eggs by the half-dozen, butter by the stick, coffee by the pound.

I discovered, serendipitously, that one quick way to store bedding in a Westfalia camper set-up is simply to roll it up towards the rear, then turn the bed into a seat for day cruising. When I arrived at my destination late at night, the bedding had been warmed up on the rear deck behind the seat. It was a pleasure to fold down the seat, unroll the sleeping bag, and sleep in a pre-heated bed.

In the months before we set up the shop at Deep Creek Lake, Bob had also moved his main school and factory from Libertyville to Hampstead, just north of Baltimore. The Deep Creek Lake operation wasn't making money, so we suspended it for the winter and moved back to the Baltimore area. Bob could pay me only about a hundred dollars a month during the fall months. I couldn't rent an apartment for that money, so Bob made a suggestion: live at the shop, in my bus. I could pull it into the shop at night, and move it back out in the morning. I could store my food in the shop refrigerator, and use the shop restroom for washing up. I accepted the offer, more out of ego than anything else. I wasn't ready to acknowledge the fact that the move into the hang gliding business had been a mistake, and that the logical thing to do was to go back into the civil service, get a steady paycheck, and forget about the hang gliding industry.

There were two strong arguments for living in the bus. First, I knew from the previous summer's experience that I could do it, as long as my needs remained simple. Second, I couldn't afford an apartment on what Bob was paying me. He was having enough trouble putting a roof over his family's head and food on their table on the slim revenue that the shop was bringing in over the winter, when most of our training hills were unuseable.

I passed the fall in that fashion in relative comfort, plugging a small electric heater into the bus's AC outlet and connecting an extension cord from the shop's mains to the bus. Of course, such comfort would have been impossible if an army of friends hadn't been willing to loan me the use of their showers during that time. Blanche Dubois might have relied on the kindness of strangers; I depended heavily on the generosity of friends. So I might as well take the time here to formally thank Bob, Craig, Don, Gail, Judy, Margie, Marie, Ron, Tom, Weegie, and a handful of others whose names I've forgotten in the intervening three decades.

In December, Bob formally "laid me off" (in the sense that he said that there was no longer any money to pay me). I drove down to Florida and spent that winter with my parents. A short-term job with the Polk Company allowed me to rebuild my financial resources. I took advantage of my father's hospitality to commandeer his garage, where I took off all the CV joints and re-packed them with grease. That was by far the messiest repair I

53

have ever done on a car, and if I have to have it done again, I'll gladly pay somebody else to do it.

In the spring, Bob called to tell me that the business was again making money, he was re-activating his dreams of a hang gliding school at the Wisp ski area, and he needed me as an instructor there. I drove back to Maryland, and Bob and I headed back to Deep Creek Lake. There was no money for a campground this year, so we camped in the meadow behind the skeet shop — me in my camper, and Bob and his family in a new, larger pop-up trailer. I cooked all my meals in the bus and used the toilet facilities in the ski lodge. When I needed to take a shower, I headed up the road to Grantsville, where some old friends of mine were renovating a hundred-year-old hotel on the old Cumberland Trail.

At the end of the summer, Bob admitted defeat. The tourist base to support a school just wasn't there, and the Wisp people came to regard us as a potential liability rather than a summer-time revenue-enhancer. The hundreds of dollars he and I had invested in the facility were a complete write-off. So we all went back to Hampstead and put our resources into the shop there.

The Blunder Bus became the quasi-official vehicle for Econ-O-Flight systems, even more so than Bob's Datsun B-210 station wagon. It was the Blunder Bus that usually transported the school gliders to the training hill, along with the helmets, harnesses, and all the other paraphernalia we needed. I had built a roof rack for it that could accommodate four gliders when the roof was raised, and up to eight when the roof was lowered. And it was the bus that all the students followed, like a line of chicks follows its mother, as we traveled through the countrysides of Maryland, eastern Pennsylvania, and northern Virginia. It was not uncommon for me to lead a caravan of up to ten cars to the training hills. CB radios were quite the fad back then, and I had one in the Blunder Bus. If any student's car was similarly equipped, we would put that car at the rear of the caravan, so that between us we could keep an eye on potential stragglers and traffic stops. Somehow, the system worked and nobody got separated.

54

The bus came in handy in other ways. I remember one autumn day near Spring Hill, Pennsylvania, where five students and I had some gliders set up on a windswept hill. Unfortunately, the wind chose to sweep the hill in an unfavorable direction, and carried rain squalls with it as well. After an hour of huddling under the gliders and waiting for the wind to cooperate, we piled into my bus, where I fired up the Coleman stove and made hot tea and cocoa for everybody. We were able to seat all six of us inside, all cozy and out of the weather. I can't remember whether the wind eventually straightened out, dried up, and allowed us to complete the lesson, but I will never forget how my students responded to my impromptu hospitality wagon.

That autumn passed pretty much like the previous one did, with me living in my bus at the shop in Hampstead. By that time, I had accumulated about forty thousand miles on the salvaged engine and it was starting to show some wear, so I undertook my second engine overhaul, all the way down to the crankshaft, using the shop's unused assembly area for a garage. One of the other instructors, a former Honda service manager named Ron Higgs, was watching me insert the circlips that hold the piston's wrist pin in position. He came over and told me this story:

It was his custom to give his engine rebuilders all the time and space they needed to do the job. He asked only that the rebuild be perfect. To test their reliability, he would wait until the engine had been reassembled and was awaiting reinstallation. When the rebuilder took his break, Ron would walk over to the workbench and leave a single circlip there, right on the edge where it might have been laid in the course of the engine dismantling. Then he would hang around until the tech guy discovered the circlip. If the tech guy was conscientious, he would sigh deeply and start dismantling the engine again to replace the "missing" circlip, whereupon Ron would step up, reveal the prank, and congratulate him on his dedication. But if the tech threw the circlip away, Ron would hand him his walking papers instead. There would be no missing parts in any of the engines that passed through Ron's shop, regardless of the cost. I took the lesson to heart, although it cost me much time and labor in years to come; I would wonder if I had been as thorough as I could have been, and would retrace my work until I was sure. And years later, when I was foreman of a sail loft that made hang glider sails, I would hold my sailmakers to that same standard of perfection, telling them that I didn't care how long it took or how much it cost, as long as the sail was flawless.

Bob had given up trying to sell people gliders of his own design. He had come to realize, I think, that he had no real talent for design, and it would be far easier to sell the vastly superior gliders that other manufacturers were producing. I was flying many of them myself, having learned enough of the rudiments of the sport to advance to a "Hang Two" or novice level of proficiency. (The "Hang Ratings," then as now, were Beginner, Novice, Intermediate, Advanced and Master.) This was, at the time, the minimum level to be certified as an instructor by the United States Hang Gliding Association. I also test flew any glider I could get my hands on, learning about the strengths and weaknesses of the various designs.

Fall turned into winter, and it was a hard one. Snow piled up on our training hills, and instruction was impossible. The economy took a downward turn, and people for the most part stopped buying expensive toys like hang gliders. Since Bob couldn't support his family on the non-existent winter revenues of the hang glider shop, he traveled to Louisiana to work as an electrician on the oil rigs on the Gulf of Mexico, sending money back to his family. I survived on what little revenues I was making from lessons, repairs, and spare parts sales.

It was a bleak time for me, but was made a little better by a trip to Key West, Florida in December, 1977, with my girlfriend, where we stayed the night at campgrounds from North Carolina to Florida, and swam in the ocean, harvested wild coconuts, and made love in the bus at Bahia Honda in the Florida keys. I didn't know it then, but that trip would turn out to be my last extended trip in the Blunder Bus along the East Coast. (I also didn't know that my girlfriend would break up with me on Valentine's Day weekend, of all times. I still think she could have done a little better job with her timing on that.)

56

In April, 1978, Bob came back from Louisiana. He told me that he was shutting down the business, threw a couple of his personal gliders onto his car, and drove off. I had just turned thirty, and not only was I jobless, but it fell to me to tell all our customers that there would be no refunds for pre-paid lessons or deposits on gliders. A lot of people who had partial ownership in the company were out all their investments. Customers came to pick up the gliders they'd stored at the shop. I made sure that all necessary repairs were made to the gliders, charging only for parts. Over the next few days, I moved my few personal effects from the shop into my ex-wife's apartment for storage.

One of the shop's major glider suppliers was the Electra Flyer company, at that time the country's biggest hang glider manufacturer. A few days after the shop closed, I had called Ruben Baca, one of their factory managers, about the status of some gliders we had on order there. During the conversation, he told me that while our gliders were ready for shipment, we could expect future delays because they were desperately short of workers. I answered that there weren't going to be any more orders, because the shop was going out of business. "What are your plans?" he asked. I told him that I had none. Once I told him about some of the fabrication and repair work I had done over the past two years, he said that I had a job waiting for me there if I could get there within a week.

And so it was that I loaded what I could into the bus and headed west. It was my first westward journey since my Berkeley days, and it seemed fitting that I would travel west as I had traveled east, in a VW bus.

My only difficulty on that trip was when I hit terrific headwinds as I crossed into New Mexico. I found myself shifting into third gear, then into second. Thirty miles an hour is no speed to travel on an interstate highway, but I had no choice. I moved onto the shoulder and crawled along, thanking my stars that visibility was good, so that people could see me and avoid as I made my slow way down the highway. A few hours later, the winds died and I was able to make progress again. I would be very late getting into Albuquerque, where the Electra Flyer factory was located. Around midnight, I pulled into a UPS parking lot on the north side of town, drew the curtains, and slept.

The next morning, I found the factory and claimed the job. I was happy to see another VW bus in the parking lot. It belonged to Keith Nichols, a former U.S. hang gliding champion, who was now employed as a sales representative at Electra Flyer.

Over the next two years, the bus served me well in getting myself, a few friends, and our gliders up to Sandia Crest, which overlooks Albuquerque from an elevation of four thousand feet over the city. At first, I didn't have the skills to fly there myself; when the afternoon thermals start popping up from the canyons on the mountain's western face, it has a well-earned reputation of being one of the most demanding and dangerous flying sites in the world.

But every hang glider pilot usually needs somebody to drive their car and glider to the top of the mountain and to retrieve him or her in the landing area once the flight is over, and I was that somebody for a year before I took my first flight off that mountain. I chauffered some of the country's best pilots, and hung around while they set up the gliders and assessed the weather conditions. I watched their take-offs, noting where and how they made their first turn to best use the lift they were finding. It was the best learning environment possible for a novice pilot.

We also made trips to other flying sites in New Mexico, Utah, Arizona and, once, to California. My bus was no stranger to the roads of the Southwest. On the California trip, I and my friend Mike Tandysh happened to be driving through Arizona when the temperature was well over a hundred, and we had to close the vents and vent windows and swelter, because the air outside was even hotter. (As we were driving through Winslow, Arizona, Mike suddenly yelled out "Stop the car!" We stopped at the nearest street corner. Mike got out, loitered there for a minute or so, and then got back in. "Okay," he said. I understood. Everybody should have a chance to act out an Eagles song once in a while.)

In California, I dropped Mike off in L.A. and proceeded down the coast to meet Barbara Graham in San Diego. Barbara was a hang glider pilot I'd met on the East Coast, when I worked at

Econ-o-Flight. She was also a VW camper owner, and we caravanned together to some of the flying sites and hang glider factories that Southern California was peppered with at the time.

It was then that I became acquainted with a peculiar subculture that had sprung up in the factories there. At Electra Flyer, only a small minority of the workers were pilots. The rest treated their relationship with the company strictly as a job, and drove home each night to a life entirely divorced from flying. But in California's hang glider factories, the majority of workers were also pilots, who worked at the factory to obtain the latest gliders at a discount. This tended to raise hob with factory production and delivery schedules, as the entire crew might disappear when a nearby flying site became soarable. The only similar phenomenon I have ever seen, before or since, was the "hacker" culture that sprang up in the seventies and eighties, a lifestyle that encompassed both work and entertainment, where people spent more of their off-hours in the computer lab than they did at home, and where working magic with computers was all they cared about.

And it was largely for the same reason: they were creating an industry that had never existed before, and knew that the infancy of that industry was giving them an opportunity that might never come again. Why be a salesman or an accountant when you can see people take flight in a way that never happened before? What if you could help them by building wings that flew better than any wings had flown before? Advances in design were taking place almost monthly, and the only way to keep up with that breakneck progress was to keep riding the crest of the wave. If that meant forsaking the usual trappings of success for a year or two, so be it.

The hang glider businesses of the time had other traits in common with the nascent computer start-ups. There was usually no strict demarcation between the management and the workers. The people you worked with were usually the people you socialized with. Electra Flyer was the exception; the owner and office staff generally had their own social life. But in every California hang glider factory or school, there would always be some sort of company-sponsored party at some time or another

59

— dinners, barbecues, flying trips, skiing trips in winter, parties at the shop.

And there was a sense of sharing information among companies that had almost no counterpart in other industries. When somebody found a way to make a glider easier to set up or safer to fly, it wouldn't be long before those features found their way to every glider on the market. Part of this generosity was due to the fact that none of the companies was making enough money to warrant taking it to court for infringement of intellectual properties. But there was also the feeling among many of the designers that such inventions should be shared, because they improved the sport as a whole, and made hang gliding safer and more accessible to greater numbers of people. It was also a way to change the public perception of hang gliding as a high-risk sport practiced by death-defying adventurers who should maybe be prevented from hurting themselves by legislation, the force of public opinion, or both.

More often than not, the typical worker-cum-pilot had long hair, an affinity for pot, and a casual attitude toward clothes, but it would have been a mistake to label them "hippies" in the popular sense of the term. They all had jobs, and they were good at them. They generally had no use for psychedelic drugs, love beads, or property held in common. Their evangelism was reserved for hang gliding, and their goal was to fly higher, longer and farther in the most literal sense. Their jobs were a means to that goal, to allow them to buy newer and better equipment. Hard drugs got in the way of that goal, because they siphoned money and time from the true purpose of life, which was to fly.

A lot of these workers, who worked for little more than minimum wage, shared apartments or houses, dividing up the rent and, sometimes, other living expenses such as food or utilities. Some of them were "parking lot people" and every hang glider factory seemed to have a few of them. These were workers who lived in their vans at the shop as I had done in Maryland, and who no longer even had regular homes. They lived to work and to fly, and had little in the way of a social life. Electra Flyer had a prohibition on using their parking lot that way, for the very reason that other factories allowed it; the management wanted to distance itself from that culture. But California was another story.

At this point, you're surely wondering what all this has to do with Volkswagen buses. Well, I'll tell you. Probably two-thirds of the people living in the parking lots of the California factories had VW buses; the rest were living in converted delivery vans or small RVs. The buses were popular because they could transport the gliders cheaply up the mountains and around the state. There was a famous VW commercial at the time showing fifty unnarrated seconds of a Beetle driving over snowy roads. The driver pulls up to a large garage, gets out, and opens the door to reveal a snow plow. As the snow plow pulls out, the narrator says, "Did you ever wonder how the man who drives the snow plow gets to the snow plow? This one drives a Volkswagen." I often noticed several buses in a row outside a factory, each one getting loaded with gliders, and it occurred to me that VW could make another commercial where the narrator asks "Did you ever wonder how the people who fly off the mountain get to the top of the mountain?" They never did make such a commercial, of course. I doubt if VW was willing to associate its product with such a subculture. (Other car manufactures have featured hang gliders in their commercials, usually to try to invest them with the rugged spirit of adventure that sells SUVs, but Volkswagen has not been among them. As for that particular advertising slogan, Subaru eventually used it for skiers, as part of their tie-in with the Winter Olympics.)

In the winter of 1979, I decided to go back to the East Coast to visit my parents and all my old friends in Maryland. I tuned up the bus and it seemed up to the journey, so I collected a few other people who needed a ride to the East Coast, and off we went. As we were going through Kansas, I crawled into the back to get some sleep. History repeated itself, some nine years after my first cross-country bus trip — I awoke to the unmistakable sound of a blown valve.

We limped into Joplin, Missouri, where a former employee of Electra Flyer lived; Charles was now helping his father manage an auto junkyard. We pulled the engine and exposed the bad head. The valve seat was totally fried, and the head was cracked from the spark plug hole to the exhaust port. (This was the classic failure mode of that flavor of VW head.) It turned out that he had a spare head in the junkyard, with decent valve seats, but it had no valves.

I went to the auto parts store and bought some, and Charles's father showed my how to lap the valves myself with an electric drill and some abrasive compound. The procedure was to put a little grinding compound on the valve seat, slip the valve in and put the shank of the valve into the chuck of the drill. After a few minutes of grinding to seat the valve, you'd take out the valve and check your progress by applying some Prussian blue colorant to the valve seat and repeating the lapping process; when all the ink was gone, you were done. The procedure was crude and time-consuming, but it worked, and it saved us big bucks in machine-shop charges and time delays. We cleared the new-fallen snow away from the bus, re-installed the engine, and were back on the road. Once more, I was impressed with how, with a minimum of resources and a maximum of ingenuity, a Volkswagen could be kept running. No doubt there will be machinists who recoil in horror at the story I've just told. But John Muir, that high priest of on-the-road repairs, would have been proud of me.

Aside from that episode, and aside from the regular maintenance every three thousand miles and the engine overhaul I performed back in Maryland, my bus was as trouble-free as I could have hoped for. I can't remember any serious work that needed to be done to it. It was getting to be about ten years old. I had probably put about a hundred fifty thousand miles on it, on top of the sixty thousand it had on it when I bought it. I had replaced the tires a few times, the battery, a windshield wiper motor, the muffler, and the odd headlamp or two. At one point, I had to replace the clutch cable and found that the ones stocked by Volkswagen didn't fit; it turned out that my bus had been made in Brazil and required a slightly longer cable, which VW listed under a different part number. One modification I remember making was putting an amplifier between the radio and the speakers so that I could actually hear the radio over the road noise.

I also did some re-wiring of the camper area to accommodate more twelve-volt outlets and better lighting for the interior. My cleverest invention, which I still have today, was a two-step lamp using a double-filament bulb and an old headlight switch. The switch's first position, once used to regulate the amount of dimness in the dashboard bulbs, now controlled the low filament of one of the combination tail-and-brake-light bulbs. The other switch activated the high filament in the same bulb, giving me great control in the amount of light the lamp gave. The whole mechanism was encased in a Twinings Tea canister and could be hung from one of any number of convenient places in the ceiling. An extension cord would allow it to be placed up to ten feet outside the bus. I also installed a switch on the dashboard to douse my tail-lights momentarily, to signal my thanks to the truckers who allowed me to pass and scoot in front of them on the freeways.

During an off-road adventure on that East Coast trip, I backed the bus into a tree, bent the rear bumper, and left a nice little crease on the right rear quarter-panel. Resolving that would never happen again, I replaced that bumper with one made from a wooden fence-post. It stood out about a foot from the car body, which made it much easier to stand on when I was tying gliders to the roof racks on the top of the car.

By the fall of 1980, it became clear to me that I had no real possibility of moving farther up the ladder at Electra Flyer, and didn't really care for some aspects of how they managed the personnel in their factory. Their practice was to build up a staff of thirty-five to forty people in the spring and lay off all but five of them in the fall. I managed to survive those purges, but when I became foreman of the sail loft, it was part of my new duties to do the firing, and I hated to do that. So I put out some feelers for employment at some of the factories in California, where the management made more of an effort to keep their staff over the winter.

A response came back from a man named Marty Alameda, a former bull-rider who had wisely retired from the rodeo circuit at an early age. (His remarkable ability to stay on a bucking bull earned him the nickname "Flea.") Marty had fallen in love with hang gliders while on a skiing trip and, after working with Seagull Aircraft in southern California, he started a hang glider factory in his home town of Salinas, a farming community near Monterey Bay. His sail-loft foreman and chief designer, a New Zealander named Graeme Bird, was going home to resume his own manufacturing business. Marty's dealer representative, an energetic French engineering graduate named Jean-Michel Bernasconi, was eager to take over the design reins but had no interest or expertise in running a sail loft. Marty offered me the job of foreman in the fall of 1980, and I accepted. I traveled to California, driving toward the setting sun – an altogether apt circumstance, since was to be Blunder Bus's last long trip.

Thunder Bus

Thunder Bus on a hang gliding trip

When I arrived at Flight Designs, Marty was delighted to see me driving a VW bus. He had had one himself, and he told me this story:

Before Marty founded Flight Designs, he worked for Seagull Aircraft, one of the prominent hang glider manufacturers of the 1970s. Marty had a 1968 Westfalia with the pop-up roof. One fine Sunday morning, he took this bus to the Mojave Desert to do some drop-testing of a new glider. In those days, one of the ways you tested the pitch stability of a glider was to haul it up a few thousand feet with a hot-air balloon, with both the glider and its pilot dangling from the balloon's basket; the glider then disconnected from the balloon and plunged straight down into a dive. If the glider was properly designed, it pulled out of the dive after a few hundred feet of vertical descent and began flying normally. If it failed to do this, the pilot deployed a parachute connected to both him and the glider, bringing the whole thing back to earth at a reasonable descent rate. (And if that didn't work, he had a second parachute to deploy.)

The tests went without a hitch, with Trip Mellinger doing the first drop and Marty himself doing the second one. Neither one of them had to deploy any of his parachutes. The gliders were then rolled up and loaded on top of the VW bus. As they were pulling out of the parking area, the accelerator cable on Marty's bus broke.

Lesser beings would have sent one of the party out in search of a new cable, but not Marty's crew. They started looking around for something to repair the old one. They didn't have any string or baling wire, but they did have lots of sail ties – long, narrow strips of Dacron sailcloth used to bundle the wings together with the rolled-up sails.

So they tied a number of these together and tied one end to the throttle arm. Leaving the hood open, they ran their improvised rope over the hood and through the opened rear hatch of the bus into the passenger compartment. One person, stationed on the back seat, was given the job of engine room master. He tugged the cord varying amounts at the direction of the driver.

When Marty needed to accelerate, he would yell out "Ahead one third!" and the throttle man would pull the rope a bit, responding "One third, aye!"

"Ahead two-thirds!"

More of a pull. "Two thirds, aye!"

"Full speed ahead!"

Even more pull, as far as it could go. "Full speed ahead, aye, captain!"

"Stop engines!"

Slack the cord. "Stop engines, aye!"

With this verbal coordination, Marty was able to move through the gears with the engine at more or less the proper speeds, singing out the speeds to the back seat. (Fortunately, there was a lot of empty road to practice on before they got into serious traffic.) And so they proceeded, from Mojave through San Bernardino and the Los Angeles freeway system, all the way to Marty's home in Santa Monica, with Dan following in his own red and white 1970 bus and witnessing the whole enterprise.

When a managerial position opened at Flight Designs, I remembered my friend Randy Hall, who had worked with me at Electra Flyer and, in fact, had taken over my foreman job when I left that company. Randy had had his own VW bus, one of the

66

first "bay window" models, which he named the "Tragic Bus." (And he gave himself the nickname "The Road Worrier.") When the Tragic Bus's engine burned a valve, he ended up living at my house in Albuquerque for a week, hitching a ride to work with me every day and rebuilding the engine in the evenings on the back porch. He got along well with my housemates, the rebuild went pretty smoothly, and soon the bus was back on the road. "With the new rings and heads, I expect that thing to climb trees," he declared. Later that year, I moved to California, and a few months later he quit the Albuquerque job, largely for the same reasons I had, and headed for Maryland in the bus.

I gave Randy a call the following year to ask him how he was doing. It turned out that he and his girlfriend Robin weren't happy in Maryland, and when I offered him the managerial position that was open at Flight Designs, he accepted. They'd be out in a week, he said.

A week later, I got a call. He and Robin had made it as far as Dublin, California, before the Tragic Bus broke down. I can't remember what went wrong with the engine, but I had to find somebody who could tow them the remaining hundred miles or so to Salinas. A neighbor had a Jeep that could do the job, so off we went to rescue Randy and Robin.

We found them on the shoulder of westbound Interstate 580, eating cherries. Randy had a little paper American flag he was waving; he was holding it upside down, the universal signal of distress. Robin had used their waiting time to walk their wooden duck-on-a-stick, while their two real birds — a parakeet and a cockatiel — were resting comfortably in their cages in the back of the bus. Randy had used the time to compose his own parody of Loudon Wainwright's classic "Dead Skunk in the Middle of the Road:"

"Dead bus by the side of the road
Dead bus by the side of the road
Dead bus by the side of the road
Leakin' to high heaven."

Randy Hall, the Road Worrier

We made it back to Salinas, where my landlady Cynthia took pity on Randy and Robin and allowed them to sleep on her living room couches until we could find a house for the three of us to share, which we were able to do within a week or so. Marty's brother Dan had a machine shop across the street from the factory, and he gave Randy a little space and the use of his parts washer. So it was *deja vu* all over again, as Randy and I (and Robin, who was hired as a seamstress) piled into my bus each morning for work and came back each night, after which Randy would borrow my bus and return to the machine shop to work on his engine.

Not long after I rescued Randy, the transmission in the Blunder Bus started to give me problems, popping out of gear in fourth. I was able to effect a temporary cure by taping a brick to an army boot. When I shifted into fourth, I slipped the boot over the gearshift lever and counted on its weight to keep the gear engaged. But when it started popping out of some of the lower gears, I realized that it was time to replace the transmission.

I ended up replacing much more than that. One day in the spring of 1982, I lifted up the front floor mat and found myself looking at the parking lot asphalt; the floor had rusted completely through. I started lifting up the other mats, and found gaping holes; the years of driving on salt-treated eastern roads had taken its toll on the undercarriage of the bus. Even worse, it looked like rust was starting to affect those members of the frame where the steering and front suspension components of the bus were attached.

Dan Alameda came over to take a look. He told me that repairs simply wouldn't be worth it; it was questionable whether there was even enough good metal left to weld new metal onto. The Blunder Bus had come to the end of the road.

I looked around for another bus, but couldn't find one in my price range. Dan finally found a listing in the *San Jose Mercury News* for a bus for sale. The bus was a 1971, with no engine or rear bumper and some front-end damage. It was owned by a company that modified vans into RVs, but they decided they didn't want to do the modifications and repairs and were willing to let it go for six hundred dollars. Dan pointed out that I already had a serviceable engine. It was even a 1971 engine, so all I had to do was unplug that vacuum port and hook it up to the disc brake system on the new car. I drove up to San Jose to take a look at the bus, and I liked what I saw. The "front end damage" consisted of a huge dent in the front of the bus, a smashed headlight, and a bent door pillar and passenger side door. Except for that, there wasn't a spot of rust on the frame. It had been a California bus since it was new. The transmission was intact and was probably original. The tires were shot, but the ones on Blunder Bus were practically new and could be swapped over onto the rims of the other one. So I bought the bus and paid an additional fifty dollars to have it towed the sixty miles south to Salinas.

Dan allowed me two parking spaces in front of his shop to do the necessary metamorphosis. First, the bent passenger-side door came off. I got some jacks, crowbars, and hammers and, with the help of Dan's partner Gordy Siems, bent the door pillar back to where it was supposed to be. We then straightened out the front as best we could, so that Blunder Bus's right headlight assembly could be installed there and the headlight aimed properly. We hung the Blunder Bus's passenger door on the new bus, and installed the engine. We jacked up both cars, took the tires off, and had the tires switched around. Finally, I removed the wooden-fencepost bumper from the old bus and installed it in the new one. The new bus was ready to roll. We did it all in a weekend.

As a bonus, it had an "external" oil cooler mounted inside the duct that brought air from the scoops to the engine compartment; it was cooled by an additional scoop mounted on the side of the bus below the stock scoop. You used to see a lot of these oil coolers mounted on buses of that era, in several configurations of location, type of scoop, and so on.

There were two popular ways to install them: as an auxiliary unit, using piping that left the original oil cooler in place, or as a replacement for the original oil cooler. This one was one of the latter ones. The drawback was that the only time the cooler was effective was when the bus was moving at some speed, forcing air around it to cool it. (The stock oil cooler, on the other hand, sat inside the fan housing where it could be cooled by a fan that was always running when the engine was, whether the bus was parked or doing sixty miles down the highway.) Dan and Gordy advised me to use this new set-up in place of the stock system, since the bus wouldn't be in much city traffic.

Gordy, who had a high reputation for servicing and hot-rodding motorcycles, also advised me to put a high-performance muffler and a mechanical-advance distributor on the engine to give it better performance. This agreed with the advice that John Muir had given in his book, and the modifications were made. When we took the new bus around the block, it accelerated quicker, and with a throatier roar, than Blunder Bus ever had. This was going to be ... Thunder Bus!

It only remained for me to remove all the Westfalia camper components from the Blunder Bus and install it into Thunder Bus. Time prevented me from installing the pop-top roof just then, so I stored it in another building that Flight Designs was renting in the industrial park. Thunder Bus had a sliding sunroof, and I figured that I wouldn't need the pop-top until the weather turned bad. Finally, I took the spare tire bracket off the front of the old bus and bolted it onto the new bus.

It was a good thing I did, too. A few years later, I was driving down River Road outside Salinas when I hit a deer. It was just after sunset. I caught just a glimpse of him as he leapt in front of the bus, bounced off the spare tire, and tumbled off the road. I stopped the bus, took a flashlight, and went looking for him. That probably wasn't the brightest thing to do, since an injured deer can be dangerous, but I did it anyway. I couldn't find him, though; he must have come to his feet and bounded off. Maybe he had internal injuries that eventually killed him, or maybe the spare tire helped cushion the blow. I don't know. But that tire certainly saved the windshield, and possibly the entire front of the bus. After that, I became a firm believer in front-mounted spare tires, and have been ever since.

As it turned out, I never installed the pop-top. In the spring of 1982, Marty died while test flying a prototype of an ultralight aircraft he and his brother were developing. He had sold his business to the Pioneer Parachute Company in Connecticut the previous winter. Pioneer was doing nicely with government contracts (most notably the parachutes used by returning spacecraft in the space program) and with sport parachutes like the Parasail, but was looking to expand into other areas of sport aviation, particularly ultralights. It was even opening a new factory for ultralights back in Connecticut, and Randy and Robin drove back there in the Tragic Bus to run it.

Marty's death didn't stop those plans, but his freewheeling, hands-on management style was gone and the Salinas factory was no longer a pleasant place to work at. Jean-Michel Bernasconi, who had been hired as a dealer representative and was now Flight Designs' head designer, was appointed interim manager in Marty's place but was never given free rein to direct the company the way it had been run before. He now had to answer to executives in three-piece custom suits who had no sport-flying experience whatsoever, and who refused to be taught the idiosyncrasies of that particular market. When it became clear to him that he would never be able to run the company the way he liked, he left to start his own company, called Pacific Windcraft. I became his first employee, hired to staff, train, and run the sail loft.

71

Born in France, Jean-Michel had been in the country since 1978, working as a dealer representative for both Bill Bennett Delta Wing Kites and Gliders and then Marty Alameda's Flight Designs. There was hardly a single important hang glider dealer in North America that he hadn't met, and he used that list of personal contacts to enormous advantage in setting up the new company. Not only that, but Jean-Michel had designed a higher-performance glider, the Vision, that would be so easy to fly that even a novice could handle it. Flight Designs didn't want to build it, as they already had a novice glider in production as well as a higher-performance one, and felt that they could maximize profits by selling those instead. They couldn't see the ground-breaking potential of the new design, but we could.

I left Flight Designs with mixed feelings. On the one hand, these were my friends, business associates, and flying buddies. And my experience with Bob Martin's company had made me wary of start-ups and the daunting challenges they faced; I would again be gambling on whether another person's dream would really pan out, and asked myself if I wanted to ride that roller coaster again. On the other hand, it just wasn't the same without Marty. Patty Butler, my successor as sail loft manager, was a quick learner, and I had no doubt that she would be able to take over all my duties. On the one side lay security; on the other side, promise. Pacific Airwave seemed to be our best chance to keep alive the spirit of Marty's company.

I think I left just in time. Flight Designs's facilities were being cut back. When I came back to retrieve the pop-top later that year, I found that Flight Designs wasn't renting it any more, and that the building had been cleaned out. Flight Designs continued to stay in business for another few months, but soon everybody got the axe. Pioneer had only wanted the ultralight part of the operation; they kept the hang glider factory going only because Marty insisted on it as a condition of the deal. With Marty gone, the hang glider operation had no voice, and was discarded like so much packing material. Of the original Flight Designs crew, only Randy and Robin were retained, and only because they had been transferred to the new ultralight facility in Connecticut.

It turned out that I lost the use of the sliding roof as well. Jean-Michel needed to hang a sign for our new factory about fifteen feet off the ground, and parked the car next to the wall to act as a scaffold. He stepped wrong and bent the roof; after that, it would close easily but be hell to open. Since I am a very forgiving soul, nothing more was said about it, but I did miss that sliding roof. I kept my eyes open for another pop-top like the one I had, but in those pre-Internet days I had no success.

Thunder Bus was my primary mode of transportation for the next eleven years. On the whole, it gave me little trouble, except for the time that the generator died as I was going over Pacheco Pass one night. It had been showing some signs of wear, and I had even bought a kit of replacement generator brushes so I could do the repair at some convenient time. So of course, the generator chose to fail at a most inconvenient time, in the dead of night at the top of Pacheco Pass, which was at that point a four-lane highway with a guardrail, leaving only a six-foot wide shoulder. As I climbed the pass, I noticed the headlights starting to fade. Just before I reached the summit, the engine died.

I pulled over onto the shoulder, got out the flashlight and the Idiot Book, and confirmed what I suspected: the generator brushes were no longer making contact with the commutator. It turned out that Muir had a procedure for just this situation; it involved unscrewing the generator brushes from their housing, feeding them out through the slots in the generator, and polishing the commutator with some sandpaper. John's directions called for the engine to be running, but that was out of the question, so I did the best I could by polishing what I could see, rotating the generator shaft a few degrees with a socket wrench, and repeating the procedure. As I was doing this, other cars and trucks were whizzing by me in the slow lane, close enough to my crippled bus to set it rocking. It was a long, exasperating job, but I finally got the new brushes installed. It now remained only for me to somehow get the bus rolling down the hill and "pop-starting" the car by throwing it into gear to crank the engine. I had done this before, with this and other cars, but never in reverse.

I waited for a lull in the traffic, enough to ensure that I would have the slow lane to maneuver in. Ignition on, parking brake released, tranny in reverse, clutch in ... and I rolled backwards down the hill. The speedometer still read zero (speedometers don't display reverse speeds, I realized), but when I got up to maybe six or seven miles an hour, I popped the clutch. It was enough, but just barely. Once started, the engine continued to run, and I waited another half an hour for the battery to re-charge. I pulled back onto the road and made for home.

Thunder Bus, like all buses, had formidable off-road capabilities, and I was used to departing from the paved road at whim. Only once did it ever get stuck off the road. Arriving late at a fly-in near Lake McClure, I took the wrong turnoff and found myself on a road that slanted sharply downward and sideways, and got mired down in loose gravel. Trying to extricate myself, I succeeded only in skidding the bus over to one side of the road, crashing into a tree and destroying the air scoop on the left side of the bus, which also happened to be the scoop that fed air to the external oil cooler. The scoop, made of a hard plastic that had been exposed to the sun for years, had shattered completely.

The next morning, I got some help and had the bus towed back to the road, but I didn't want to drive much further until the scoop was replaced; I feared that the cooler really needed that blast of cooling air to function, and if the cooler couldn't function, the engine would overheat, causing more grief than I was willing to pay for. So I thought, well, what can I do? I did have some duct tape, and a hunting knife, and there was this nearly empty can of Coleman fuel. So I fashioned a scoop out of the can and taped it to the bus. It wasn't pretty, but it got me down the hill and back to Salinas, where I replaced it with a proper one.

One day, as I was driving to work, I started hearing a noise I'd never heard before. Every fifteen seconds or so, there would be a short wail, varying in pitch. It sounded for all the world like a meowing cat. As I drove down the road, I wondered what could possibly make a noise like that. My speed didn't seem to affect the timing, nor did the RPM of the engine. It was there whether I was rolling or stopped for a light. What was weirder, the sound seemed to be coming from somewhere over my head and to my rear. After a couple of miles, I pulled onto the freeway and got up to sixty miles an hour, but the noise didn't go away, so I pulled over onto the shoulder, stopped the car, and went looking for the source of the noise. I found nothing untoward, either in the main cabin of the bus or in the engine compartment. As I got back on the road and up to speed, the noise returned, so I took the next exit and started looking again. But this time I looked up, and found the problem.

As you've probably guessed by now, the sound was caused by ... a meowing cat. A neighbor told me later that it had been in the habit of climbing onto the roof of the bus and sunning itself. Why it didn't wake up and jump off when I got in and started the bus that morning, I'll never know. But it stayed put as I drove down the street and onto the freeway. After three miles of a wild ride, it was in a state of shock, and I was able to gently pick it up and put it inside the bus. By the time I got back home, it had largely recovered its composure and was clamoring to be let out; it needed no urging to disembark once I opened the sliding door. The cat seemed none the worse for wear from its adventure, but nobody ever saw it on top of the bus again.

Eventually, the transmission started to wear. Around 1986, it began to pop out of fourth gear. Instead of the army boot and brick, I upgraded to a shock cord, one end of which was fixed to the bottom of the driver's seat. The other end was hooked to the gearshift lever just after it was moved into fourth gear, but before I re-engaged the clutch. This system worked well for a few months, but then the other gears started acting up, and I bit the bullet and had a rebuilt transmission installed by a garage in Santa Cruz.

I had the engine replaced in 1991 when it burned another valve as I was driving to Burnet, Texas. I was able to get the bus to a motel on the freeway near Casa Grande, Arizona, where I spent the night and then started calling for tow trucks in the morning. I needed to be in Burnet as soon as possible, so doing the work myself without facilities was out of the question. As it turned out, the bus was towed to a Casa Grande garage owned by a man named "Mac" McCullough. He shopped around some parts for me among the dealers in nearby Chandler and found that rebuilt engines, with reconditioned blocks and heads, could be had for around the same price he would have to charge me for a head replacement. He would be happy to let me do the work in a corner of his shop, transferring all of the non-engine parts (generator, manifolds, fuel pump, carburetor, and so on) from my blown engine to the new one. When I was finished with that, he would help me re-install the engine. For all this, he charged me not a penny in labor. And if I took longer than a day, he would take me to his house and let me sleep on his couch.

Needless to say, I took him up on this generous offer, and by the evening of the second day I was on the road again. I gave him a six-pack of the home-brewed beer I was saving for the trip. I am eternally grateful to him for turning a catastrophic vacation into a pleasant one. I made it to Burnet only three days later than I had originally planned. Mac reminded me of a truth of human nature that Kurt Vonnegut would later call "original virtue" ... that people can be pretty damn nice to each other if they want to be.

I remembered Mac on a later trip over Pacheco Pass, when I encountered a car with its hood up and a fellow looking into the engine compartment as his wife and kids stood by the side of the road. The fellow told me that a fan belt had broken. I had the wrenches and stuff to fix the car, but no fan belt for it, so he got into the bus and we drove to a service station about ten miles down the road, bought a new belt, drove back, and had it on his car within an hour of my stopping. He wanted to give me twenty dollars, but I told him to "pay it forward" by passing the favor on to somebody else.

But I think it was on that trip to Texas that my attitude toward Volkswagen buses fundamentally changed. I didn't like breaking down by the side of the road anymore. I wondered what it would be like to drive a vehicle that I didn't have to get out and fix occasionally. I no longer needed the bus as a camper, because I had become a tentmaker by that time and people were expecting me to be camping in my products, and not in my bus. (And, to be sure, the only way I could ensure that my tent

76

designs were superior was to test them continually and note where improvements had to be made.) So I bought a Volvo station wagon, and then a Toyota pickup truck with a shell, to schlep my tents and camping stuff around.

But that was the bite of the apple that opened my eyes to a new world. The Volvo was a superlative driving machine — quiet, speedy, solid, quick to accelerate, easy to steer, able to hold the road at whatever speed or conditions it was asked to meet.

But I couldn't let the bus go, just yet. I parked it outside the factory at Pacific Airwave (the successor company to Pacific Windcraft) and used it as a sort of private break room, where I could eat lunch and smoke a cigarette in peace. One day, Jean-Michel's daughter Collette found me there and told me, "John, I wish you wouldn't smoke." Now people had been telling me that for years without result, but when it's coming from a ten-year-old girl, it becomes a different matter. I suddenly recalled smoking around my own teenage sister when I was in my twenties, and I wondered if my habit hadn't influenced her to take up the habit. On top of that, my mother was suffering from years of smoking, becoming more emphysemic by the year, and her circulatory system was being further ravaged by the onset of diabetes. She needed to quit smoking and I realized that it was time for me to quit, too. If we had to suffer, we would suffer together.

Ironically, kicking the cigarette habit was the thing that finally made me get rid of the bus. After I quit smoking, the smell of tobacco would make me ill, and the bus positively reeked of tobacco from a decade of smoke. I could no longer sit in it without getting a headache. I finally decided to get rid of the bus, since I could no longer drive it around.

It was about five months after I'd given up smoking that I finally cleaned out the bus for the last time. By that time, I was largely free of the addiction that dominated my life for the previous twenty-five years. While cleaning out the compartment under the passenger seat, I found a pack of cigarettes that had somehow slipped down there years before. I remembered the many frantic nights when I'd run out of smokes and the stores weren't open; if I known that those cigarettes were there a year ago, I would have torn the bus apart to find them, I thought with a smile. Then I threw the pack away.

For years, Jean-Michel had been pleading with me to sell the bus, but when the time came to part with it, I found that, with its misshapen nose and non-matching body panels, it had zero resale value. So I sold it for scrap, getting probably fifty dollars for it. When my buddies heard I was getting rid of the bus, two other bus owners asked me for parts. Somebody (I think it was Toni Kwalick) got the engine I put in during my Texas trip. The wooden bumper was greatly admired by a Pacific Airwave employee from Nicaragua named Hernando (or "Airnando," as we called him). "Now that's a *bomper!*" he would say. When I got rid of the Thunder Bus, he pleaded with me to give him the bomper, so I did. He drove his newly bompered bus back to Nicaragua, where it caught fire and burned to the ground, bomper and all.

The next day, the bus was towed away, and my Volkswagen days were over. Or so I thought.

PART TWO: George

I Meet George

June 21, 2008

Back in the nineteenth century, it was the custom of lonely settlers and prospectors to order brides through the mail. The groom-to-be would look through a catalog showing prospective wives and send a candidate some money and a proposal. If all went well, he would send more money for her to travel to where the couple would meet. If the pair decided that they would be compatible (a decision forced as much by desperation, financial straits, and hard-nosed pragmatism as by romance), the knot would be tied.

I can imagine such a settler waiting anxiously for the destined fiance to step off the train, or the boat, or the stagecoach, or whatever. Which one is she? What would she look like? What does her voice sound like? Will she be the one for me? Or would this turn out to be the biggest mistake of my life?

I feel a little like that guy right now. I have arranged to buy a bus, sight unseen, from a fellow in Los Angeles. For once in my life, I had a few thousand dollars to spare and did some looking around for older buses. Just pricing them, you understand. No real intention to buy. I checked some of the on-line resources, and the sort of camper-bus I had in mind seemed to be going for between five and ten thousand dollars. I went so far as to check out a few buses in the flesh, so to speak, kicking the tires, looking around inside, asking price, and trying to imagine how the bus would fit into my life-style. And then I made the fatal mistake of visiting eBay Motors.

If I had been smart, I would have stopped with the "finished auctions" section the web site, showing completed transactions along with details such as pictures, descriptions, and the final price established. But I thought that since I was there, I'd check out what was currently on the block for auction.

And there it was. A 1971 camper with 196,000 miles on it, with about thirteen pictures of it in various configurations. It had a little rust at the base of the windshield, and a sizable dent in the left rear corner caused by the previous owner backing it into his other car in his driveway. It seemed clean. According to the write-up, it had a recent engine and transmission overhaul and a history of regular and diligent maintenance, backed up with complete documentation going back twenty years. Its name was George.

The $700 reserve had already been met, and the current bid was $1200, with the auction to run for another twelve hours. "What the hell," I thought. "I'll put a bid on it for a little over three thousand dollars, and see what happens." To my surprise, I became the high bidder, raising the price to just over $1500. That told me that the previous bidder had specified that he would go no higher than $1500. At around 8:30 that night, I found that I had been outbid, raised my bid to a little over $4500, and again became the high bidder at around $3500. When I went to bed that night, the auction had two hours to go and the bidding hadn't changed. Usually, these auctions see a flurry of last-minute bidders, each trying to squeeze in the high bid at the latest possible second. So I fully expected to wake up the next morning to find my puny bid dwarfed by the $8000 or $9000 that this car would surely bring.

But that didn't happen. Instead, I found that I had won, with the last bidder dropping out at $4100. George was mine.

I should have been happy and I guess I was, but the feeling alternated with a dread that I might have made a costly mistake. Sure, the price was right, but what if the bus didn't match the description? What if it wasn't quite the cream puff it was advertised to be? I emailed the seller my telephone number, and waited.

The email was answered by Marc, the seller's son. He called that same day, and we made arrangements to make contact when I flew down there. If the description was accurate, the bus would be in good enough shape to drive the four hundred miles back to Sacramento, but I brought a tool kit and a sleeping bag along, just in case.

When I was a boy, I started having flying dreams, where I would be walking along and suddenly finding myself gaining buoyancy – each step became longer, each bound became higher,

81

and I would find myself floating over the countryside. I had those dreams right up to the time I started flying hang gliders and actually had the experience of taking a few steps and finding myself airborne and gliding over the terrain. Then the dreams stopped. When I stopped flying hang gliders twenty years later, the dreams started again.

For the past year, I'd been having bus dreams, where I find myself driving a bus down a long country road, on the way to some ill-defined destination. I wondered if those dreams would stop when I started driving buses again.

The following Monday, I was on a Southwest Airlines shuttle from Sacramento to Bob Hope Airport in Burbank. The flight down took a little over an hour. I'd checked a suitcase containing a sleeping bag, a Phase I tool kit, and the Idiot Book. Marc picked me up and drove me to Grenada Hills, where I met George.

George turned out to be not such a bargain after all. The rust under the windshield turned out not to be surface rust, but went all the way through the metal. The windshield gasket had deteriorated to the point where it could no longer keep a seal, and water had entered underneath it and eaten so much of the metal away that fitting a new gasket, or a new windshield, might have been impossible. I wouldn't know until I got into it with a wire wheel. In other areas, there was a dented left rear fender that had pushed the left tail-light out of alignment and damaged the scoop, under which sat an external oil cooler. I knew about the dent, but not the oil cooler. As I explained earlier, these external coolers had been once considered indispensable additions to the engine, although there were mechanics who thought that they were more trouble than they were worth, particularly if their installation required the removal of the stock oil cooler positioned inside the fan housing. I didn't know yet what sort of hook-up this thing had.

Marc's father Jack, the bus's owner, had told me that the tires were old and needed replacing, even though they had plenty of tread. He also told me that the gas gauge didn't work. He was right on both counts. I wasn't too worried about the gas gauge. The Pink Bus didn't even have a gas gauge, and I religiously monitored the mileage on the odometer to calculate when I would next need gas. I didn't worry about the tires, either; I figured that if I could get another four hundred miles out of them, I could have them replaced in Sacramento. Little did I know.

I did a test drive and found the engine responsive and the transmission and clutch smooth. (Jack said that they had been reconditioned about five thousand miles ago). To my surprise, I found myself using the clutch and shifter as skillfully as ever, even though it had been years since I drove a stick shift. (A second surprise came when I reached home and was driving in my Toyota Sienna, and found my left foot searching for a clutch pedal that wasn't there.)

I collected all the papers and the title, gave Marc a certified check for $4150 made out to his father, and off I went.

I had to go back to the airport to pick up my suitcase, which had been put on a later flight, and then navigated my way out of Los Angeles. The weather was hot, and I was sorely tempted to take the bus up the Pacific Coast Highway, but I remembered from past trips on that road that service stops and garages were few and far between. Better to drive over the Grapevine and take State Route 99 back to Sacramento, where there were towns spaced about thirty miles apart all along the route. It would be a hotter drive, but it would be freeway all the way. This decision proved to be crucial in the hours to come.

I had been on the road for an hour when the right rear tire lost tread, making a fearful racket. The adventure was just beginning.

I was able to drive, very slowly, to the next town, which was Castaic. There I stopped in a shopping center parking lot and changed the tire with the spare. This got me another fifteen miles up the road before the spare blew in the same way. With only three good tires, I was stopped cold.

I called AAA on my cell phone and was connected with the Southern California Auto Club, who sent a flat-bed tow truck out for me. The tow truck arrived an hour later, hauled me aboard, and back we went to a business in Castaic called Benny's Tire and Road Service. I sat there among the bald, de-treaded tires, each one a sad story to which I was going to add two or three

83

stories of my own. It turned out that the left rear tire was starting to de-tread like the others had. The two front tires looked good, but were of different sizes. One of them happened to be the same size as the new tires, so that one was retained as a spare. I showed the manager (presumably Benny himself) the page in the VW owners manual that described the necessary load rating, and he said he had four such tires in stock, and I bought them. When I tried to start the bus again, it wouldn't start. I noticed that the generator belt was loose and tightened it up. A few minutes on a little buzz-box charger allowed me to get the car started again. An hour and three hundred dollars later, I was out the door with four new tires.

I drove for another three hours, driving through Bakersfield at dusk. The lights worked, thank God, although the dimmer solenoid was wonky and sometimes the dimmer switch would work and sometimes not. One more thing to log on the repair sheet. I also found out that the cigarette lighter didn't work. This disturbed me, even though I hadn't smoked in fifteen years, because I had no way to re-charge my cell phone. But my trust in George, which had taken a tremendous hit in Castaic, was beginning to return, bit by bit. I made it to a rest stop just south of Tulare, crawled into the back of the bus, and converted the seat into a bed. I slept fitfully, awakened by the trucks as they rolled through.

In the morning, the bus wouldn't start. My newly-regained trust in George was now at zero. I called Triple-A again. Waiting for the road service people to show up, I dismantled the aftermarket scoop on the right side of the bus, exposing the terminals of the battery. (For some reason, the pedestal on which the oil cooler sits had been replaced by a sort of scaffold which effectively blocked access to the battery terminals.) A fellow named Sean drove up in a tow truck to jump-start me, but the car died almost immediately upon being taken off the charging circuit. So he towed me to Tulare and dropped the van off at Camara's Auto Service Center on south K Street, which used to be part of the original State Route 99 before they built a bypass. It took some time for the only mechanic willing to work on an air-cooled Volkswagen to take a look at the car, but I was in no hurry. I hadn't had breakfast, it was about ten o'clock, and I was hungry. So I left the garage and found a fast food place a few blocks away to buy breakfast.

When I got back, I found that the mechanic still hadn't gotten to my car, so I sat in the waiting room for another hour. Still no news. The mechanic had gone to lunch, and would look at the car when he came back. Fair enough. I had been hungry enough that morning not to wish anybody a similar fate. He came back to work at one. Before he'd taken off for lunch, he'd put the battery on a charger, and the charge had failed to take. So we decided that the battery was junk. He replaced it, I paid him, and I was on the road again at two-thirty.

The rest of the trip was blessedly uneventful. I arrived in Sacramento at eight in the evening, having dawdled over dinner at an In-n-Out burger shop in Salida in hopes of missing the rush-hour traffic in Stockton and Sacramento. At that stop, I had been accosted by a burly fellow named John, who had the look of a biker, with his sleeveless leather vest and long hair gone grey. He asked me about where I got the van, how much I paid for it, what sort of mileage I was getting, what the inside was like. I realized that vans like this were becoming so rare that a lot of people might not have seen them up close before, at least not for a while. I also remembered that VW owners and bikers used to have some affinity for each other, each getting around by means of loud air-cooled engines that they often worked on themselves. He said that he'd been wanting to buy one of them for years, and had finally gotten a workman's compensation check that would pay for it. I gave him the phone number of a garage owner in Sacramento who had five or six of the things for sale.

I learned a few things about myself on that trip. First, I learned about how it was to be tired and hungry again, and how what was inconvenient at thirty years of age was downright unbearable at sixty. I also learned that I was getting too old to trust a "Phase 1" tool kit and the Idiot Book to repair my way out of trouble, as I had done so easily in my youth. Now, as I studied the engine with wrench and screwdriver in hand, it occurred to me that I no longer wished to repair my way out of trouble. It was one thing to putter around with the furnishings of the camper, and quite another to come face to face with oil, dirt, and disaster.

I also came to realize that Marc and Jack hadn't really been intentionally dishonest with me on the condition of the car. It's just that they had seen it age over thirty years. George was like that wife you married a long time ago who has gained a bit of weight over the years and dyes her hair to hide the gray but who, in your mind's eye, is still the girl you went to the prom with.

But I was seeing George in a different light now. I was not sure I wanted to undertake the necessary steps to restore him to glory, particularly with the damaged body and rusted front. Instead, the thought of removing the Dormobile top and the Westfalia furnishings and putting them into a modern minivan seemed increasingly attractive.

For the rest of this chapter, I'm simply going to quote from the journal I kept at the time. It starts a few weeks after I brought George home.

July 13, 2008

I've finally gotten the title transferred over to my name and put the bus on our insurance policy. Today, I am taking a good look over the bus, noting what works and what doesn't, and what things should be fixed in what order. Tomorrow, I'm taking the bus over to the Kombi Haus, the Sacramento garage that specializes in Transporters, and it will be interesting to see how their list compares with mine.

First, I inventory what's in the car. Jack McNeil was an inveterate list maker, and I come across a checklist for the cargo of the bus when it's set up for camping. It lists over a hundred fifty items, from basic tools and spare parts to the required types of clothing ("shirts: long sl. flannel; long sl. wool; short sleeve; tee"), and includes slingshots, sleeping bags, mousetraps, charcoal, and various types of camp furniture. I thought I carried a lot of stuff in my buses, but my list pales beside Jack's. Of course, most of this had been removed from the bus by the time I first saw it. (When I picked up the bus in June, I found an inflatable rubber raft, complete with paddle, rolled up and stashed atop the coat closet; this I gave to Marc.)

Each item in Jack's list corresponded with a location or compartment in the camper where the item is to be stored. And in each of these compartments, from the glove compartment in the front to the storage space behind the coat closet, there is a list of each item that should be in that compartment. Most of these compartments were now empty, cleaned out by Marc, but I was still astonished to find eight quarts of oil in that last-named compartment, along with a drop cloth, insect repellent, a bicycle tire pump (broken), a compass, a space blanket, a two-ampere battery charger, two canteens, a small pry-bar, a tow rope, six road flares, a nearly empty can of starter fluid, an unopened bottle of brake fluid, a similarly unopened bottle of STP, a four-ounce bottle of 90-weight oil for the transmission, several bags of tire patching kits and tools, a tire tube, a brown sock, two backpacks, and a wooden stick sixteen inches long and painted white whose purpose I could only imagine. There was also an oil bottle labeled "STP." It was empty, but its contents could be found saturating a good portion of the previous items. These went into the trash.

Behind the driver's seat was a pocket-sized repair guide for the Volkswagen Transporter published by Peter Russek. It turns out to be for buses made after 1972, so its usefulness would have been limited, since Volkswagen changed to a vastly different engine that year. Tucked inside there's a notebook labeled "Van Maintenance Notes," more evidence of Jack's penchant for lists. it contains twenty-two pages of handwritten notes listing maintenance schedules, timing specifications, diagrams showing the location of the adjustment mechanisms, and on and on ... a mini repair manual of its own. There's also a four-ounce rock. Another mystery. Was it put there by Marc, when he was a boy? Could it have been the sort of prize possession a small child would have treasured and hidden away?

Behind the passenger seat is a packet of forms put out by the County of Los Angeles, on what to do if you're involved in an accident. It looks old. One form shows that it was last revised in

1970; another bears no date, but came from the Sandia Corporation and mentions only New Mexico law. There's also a frying pan.

The glove compartment is empty except for some fuses, a pencil, a clothespin, a chart showing what fuses are for which devices, and a stack of receipts from a transmission repair place and some tire stores. All the receipts are from the 1980s.

I open the Dormobile top and two partially completed hornet's nests drop out. They have obviously been there for a long time, and the makers are no longer in residence. There are two vents in the roof, but their sealing gaskets have disintegrated. There are also two glass windows, and the seals have cracked from years of exposure. One vent refuses to close, and I can't see why. I'll have to get up there with a ladder and see what's what. There are two child-size cots built into the roof. The fabric on one of them is ripping, and the other is probably not far behind. Other than that, the top seems to be in pretty good shape, with the fabric of the bellows still intact. There is no seal around the perimeter of the roof, where it interfaces with the body of the bus, and no evidence that there ever was one. That explains how the wasps got in.

I check the fluids. The windshield washer reservoir is low, so I top it off and pressurize it with a bicycle pump. The pressure holds, but there is no spritz on the windshield when I press the button inside the wiper switch, so there's a plug in that line somewhere. The brake fluid reservoir is also low, so I top that off. The dipstick in the engine is pulled; it reads a half a quart low.

In the engine compartment, I notice that the pedestal on which the air filter sits is missing; in its place is a homebuilt sort of miniature scaffold that serves the same purpose, but blocks access to the battery. I wonder if it's worth it to have another pedestal bolted or welded into place, or simply replace the old "oil bath" filter with a paper filter that sits on top of the carburetor and eliminates the need for a pedestal altogether. I also notice that the battery is sitting on a piece of board, and that the floor underneath the board has been eaten away, presumably by battery acid over the years.

It's getting really warm now, so I knock off for the day. As I'm showering, I reflect once again on how Jack would make countless lists of innumerable items, and take the trouble to copy out in longhand every essential procedure and when it should be performed, yet be so oblivious to the serious damage that rust was doing to the windshield area and the floor of the battery compartment. Tom and Ray Magliozzi, in their radio show *Car Talk*, sometimes referred to the sudden loss of interest in maintenance that is exhibited by somebody who has had their car for a long time. After a while, door locks don't get fixed, dings don't get pulled out, cracked windows don't get replaced. The Magliozzi brothers named the phenomenon "killing the car;" it's the visible manifestation of an unconscious desire to justify getting a replacement. I wonder if Jack had reached that stage at some point. Or maybe it was one of those things that he really intended to take care of at some point, but was prevented from doing by his increasing infirmities.

Whatever the cause, there's a lot of rehab to do. Aside from what I've listed above, I've found that the high/low beam relay sticks. The driver's side door lock sometimes jams. The wood-panel headliner in front has sagged, warped, and rotted in places, and needs to be replaced. The pump that delivers drinking water from the tank is broken. The gas gauge doesn't work, and when I peek behind the dashboard to discover why, I find that there's been some aftermarket addition to it ... possibly an oscillator, meaning that the gauge isn't for a '71 bus but a later one, which in turn means that the sender in the tank could be the wrong one for the year, too. The shocks are shot, and need to be replaced. The radio works, but not well. The roof seal for the Dormobile top is completely missing, the vent seals are deteriorated beyond redemption, and the window seals leak and chalk off as I rub on them, leaving ugly black smears on my fingers. The turn signals don't cancel. The fresh-air and heater knobs have all fallen off their levers and are so hopelessly mangled that I don't know if they're salvageable. The passenger side mirror doesn't keep its adjustment and will have to be replaced. George is not in good shape, but if the parts are still available, he should be repairable. All it will take is money.

George Before Me

According to the information decoded from its M-plate, Volkswagen #2312205040 came off the assembly line on March 3rd, 1971. It's not clear whether that was the date that its chassis was finished and it was ready to be sent to the Westfalia factory in Rheda-Wiedenbrück, in the state of North Rhine-Westfalia, for conversion into a camper, or whether it marked when the conversion was complete and it was ready to be picked up. The invoice from the VW factory itself is dated May 27, 1971, and made out to one "A Mehlman."

I interviewed Mehlman's widow Jewel in 2009, and found that Albert Mehlman was a forty-five-year old schoolteacher with a wife and two teen-aged children when he bought the bus. A graduate of the University of California at Los Angeles, he taught government and history at Woodrow Wilson High School in east Los Angeles, after a short stint as a social worker. He would hold that teaching post for the entire thirty-four years of his career in public education. Jewel was born in New York City and, even though she had spent her entire adult life in California, her speech still retained a trace of the accent of the middle-class New York Jewish community of her childhood. She was a high-school teacher herself, teaching English at a number of area high schools before assuming the title of assistant principal before her retirement. She met Al at UCLA, and they were married in 1949. She described Al as a "sweet, gentle man" at numerous times during our interview; it was plain that she was still in love with him, long after his death from a stroke in 2006, at the age of seventy-nine.

Al and Jewel embraced education not only as careers but in the rearing of their children. In 1969, the family traveled to Europe for the first time, buying a Westfalia camper in Montebello and arranging to pick it up at in Europe, tour the continent, and then ship the bus back home. They were no strangers to auto-touring, having traveled extensively across the United States in a station wagon, camping along the way. The bus they bought in 1969 was an off-white Westfalia camper. It would have been one of the first of the second-generation "bay window" models,and was probably equipped with the standard Westfalia pop-top roof.

Their children participated as much in the planning of the itinerary of the trips as they did. Larry and Felicia would be given a map and told to pick out some place they wanted to go, and that stop would be included. That, of course would encourage them to research where they ought to go, and what part of European history they wished to explore. Felicia recalls those days with pleasure, saying that it was a learning opportunity that very few children get to experience.

They enjoyed the first trip so much that they did it again two years later. This time, they ordered a 1971 bus, with the same interior arrangement as their earlier one, but without the pop-up roof supplied by Westfalia at the time. That bus was George, although that wouldn't be his name at first.

The roof that Al wanted was made by a British company named Martin Walter for its own line of "Dormobile" campers. The Dormobile was one of post-war Europe's first outfitters of campers. The story goes that when the head of Martin Walter took the ferry that crossed the English channel between Dover and Calais, he noticed that there were many people sleeping in their cars in the ferry company's parking lot – vacationing families, traveling salesmen, and the like – and thought there might be a market for cars with sleeping accommodations built right in. His first Dormobile was based on the Vauxhall Bedford CA van, whose roominess would accommodate a double bed with ease. (The name came from the French "dormir" meaning "to sleep" plus "automobile.") The Dormobile was introduced in 1954, and was an immediate hit with salesmen and, later, with tourists and camping families. Later models included a stove and, most distinctively, a raise-able clamshell roof. This camper package was eventually used on a variety of motor vehicles, from the Land Rover to the commercial vans such as the Ford Transit, the VW bus, the Toyota Hi-Ace (a small commercial van never sold in the US), and even the Fiat 850T or "Familiare," which looked like a bus but was 5/6 the size. In the popular mind, a Dormobile wasn't really a Dormobile without that roof.

It is this raisable clam-shell roof that interests us here, because it was, and still is, the most distinctive characteristic of Volkswagen #2312205040. Made of fiberglass, it sported two glass skylights and two openable vents made of opaque plastic. This arrangement, along with its ability to increase headroom by over three feet beyond what the van offered from the factory, gave it an airiness that campers with other roofs lacked. Even tall people could stand inside, and there was abundant daylight (which could be modulated by curtains fitted to the skylights). It was also unique in that it opened sideways, with its hinge along the long axis of the vehicle rather than straight up (as was common with most campers of the time) or at its front or rear, as the later Westfalias did. You could spot a Dormobile roof a quarter of a mile away. As a bonus, the roof came with two fold-out cots to accommodate two diminutive people, so the double bed wouldn't have to be shared with the kids.

A lot of customers liked the roof, but preferred the camper package offered by other outfitters. By the 1960s, the company (which had changed its own name to Dormobile) began offering its roofs to other camper builders, and Volkswagen was one of them. Until 1970, you could order a Westfalia from Volkswagen with either the Dormobile or Westfalia roof.

Al and his son Larry went down to the VW dealership in Montebello and ordered a 1971 Westfalia to be picked up by the customer in Europe. And with this transaction accomplished, #2312205040's future was set.

Al was one year too late to order his Westfalia with the Dormobile top, but there was a solution: he could order it as a "tin top" Westie, without the pop-up roof, and have a Dormobile top installed by a private garage. [5]

I am grateful to Jewel and her daughter Felicia for providing me with a copy of the detailed journal that Al kept of that trip. It

---

[5] This would not have been unusual at the time, because there were a number of companies that provided these services. After my father bought a Citroën ID-19 in 1961, he took it to a coachworks in Frankfurt to have a *Schiebedach,* or sliding cloth sun-roof, installed.

relates that they picked up the car, without a pop-up roof, in Amsterdam at a VW distributorship called Autopon – the name coming from its owner, the same Ben Pon who dreamed up the concept of the VW bus in the first place. From there, they drove to the coachworks in nearby Almelo. The Dormobile top was waiting for them at the coachworks, and was installed in time for them to leave at the end of the following day. We know about this, and about their adventures with the bus over the following two months, from the meticulous record that Al kept. He noted the mileage each night, the car's maintenance stops, every step of their itinerary, how much they paid for bread and potatoes, how long it took to find campgrounds and the people they met there. He described the types of roads they encountered and the red tape they dealt with at each border. A dispassionate reader of the diary might come away from it with one of two impressions. He could revel in the encounters with local customs and mores, and the descriptions of landscapes of breathtaking beauty, and resolve to take a trip of their own. Or he would read of the constant struggle with languages, short-changing by cashiers, inferior medical facilities, and a never-ending litany of troubles cashing traveler's checks, collecting mail, and exchanging money, and vow to never set foot beyond his own borders.

The record shows that the Mehlmans seldom had a dull day and generally enjoyed their vacation, although they probably would rather have skipped their encounter with Rumanian medicine, where two of their party were hospitalized for a few days. (Jewel told me about the unsterilized spoon that served as a communal tongue depressor and was passed from patient to patient. Apparently, it is a story she has told often and with pleasure.) But they pressed on, completing a wide circuit that included Belgium, Germany, Denmark, Sweden, Finland, Russia, Romania, Bulgaria, Turkey, Greece, Albania, Yugoslavia, Italy, Switzerland, France, and Holland again — almost eight thousand miles in seven weeks. And that doesn't count a week-long side trip by air to Israel (which Jewel describes as being the high point of that trip), or the many hours of travel by ferry.

When I got home after visiting Jewel, I sipped wine and read Al's journal, following their progress in a Kümmerly & Frey

European road atlas that I kept from my late father's estate. (It bears no copyright date, but Dad must have bought it in the 1960s, during the time my own family did much of its European touring, so I presume that it shows the same major thoroughfares and ferry routes that the Mehlmans used.) Traveling vicariously with them in this fashion, I got to know them well, and regretted that I never met Al or Larry in person. Al was a better chronicler than he knew. I was impressed at the freedom he gave his children to explore and sight-see on their own, always trusting them to be able to stay out of trouble and rejoin the family on schedule. In my mind's eye, I saw Al fretting about mail deliveries at a succession of American Express offices, "Lar" forever looking for cigars and copies of the *New York Herald Tribune*, "Lish" staying back at camp to read or write letters, "J" (or "Mom") exploiting every shopping opportunity that came her way.

As they traveled, they bought various equipment, such as a tent, bought in the town where the Westfalia-Werke was, implying but not proving that it was the one that Westfalia offered as an option for the bus at the time. (They presumably retained that tent for use with their next bus, since the next owner never saw it.) They also purchased several inflatable pillows, a single-burner stove, a lantern, some cots, and a roof rack to haul the assortment of stuff. Al wrote of his delight with the camper and its Dormobile top, although he noted that it really wasn't big enough for four grown people, despite the number of beds; without the tent, the trip would have been much harder. The kids evidently used the cots only twice: once when the weather was too inclement to put up the tent, and once when they loaned the tent out to some visiting friends.

At the conclusion of their tour, Al and Larry put the bus on a boat in Bremen for stateside delivery. When the family picked it up from the importer after their return flight, it became one of their daily drivers, joining the '69 bus. (With four licensed drivers in the household, they needed all the wheels they could get.) That fleet was added to in 1973, when, on their final European tour, they would buy a bright orange camper, pick it up, and drive through the British Isles. (Jewel told me later that driving a

94

bright orange bus through the countryside of Ireland was probably not the wisest thing they did, since that color was closely identified with Northern Ireland, and animosities between the two countries still ran deep.) For that trip, Larry brought his girlfriend to accompany him. They kept the '73 for a while, taking it for trips around California, but they would no longer return to Europe to buy a new one.

The following year, Larry died in a SCUBA diving accident, eleven days after Al and Jewel's twenty-fifth wedding anniversary. He was twenty-one years old. His mother talked of her son's death with sadness, even after thirty-five years. When she told me the story, I told her about my own friends who had died long before their time, in hopes of making a connection, but I don't think I really succeeded. Her grief was still very acute, and very personal, and I had to respect that. (It is possible that the recent loss of Al, less then three years before I interviewed her, might have revived the grief for her son's passing.) I later found a picture, taken in 2003, of Al and Jewel meeting the recipients of the scholarship they had set up in Larry's name at the University of California in Irvine. In the picture, Al is tall and slender, and looks twenty years younger than he actually was. It is not hard to picture this active, vital man as he shepherds his family around Europe and describes in his journal what he sees. Here is a man who knew how to enjoy life. I think I would have liked him.

After Larry died, Al and Jewel sold the '71 bus. The buyer was Jack MacNeil, a civil engineer in Los Angeles. He was forty-seven years old. He and his wife had two children, ages thirteen and fourteen, and they bought the bus to tour the US. His son remembers Jack paying something like $4500 for it, which was, ironically, about the same as I paid Jack for it. It was Jack, or rather his children, who gave the bus its name of "George." It was intended as a mnemonic for the three letters of the license plate, where "EHG" stood for "Extra Helpful George." (There have been times when I thought that "Excedrin Headache George" would have been more appropriate, but those times have become mercifully been less frequent over the years.) Once a bus has had a name for over thirty years, to consider changing it would seem to show a profound disrespect for tradition, so George it has been for me, too.

Jack's son Mark wrote me a letter in which he shared his memories of the bus. The first big trip in it, he said, was to the World's Fair in Spokane, Washington. The route took them through Bishop, Lake Tahoe, and Reno, and thence through Oregon to Spokane and ultimately Vancouver, British Columbia. They then returned to Los Angeles, following the Pacific coast roads. "It was a long journey for us," Marc recalled, "and I can remember days of my Sister and I sitting on top of all the stuff in the back waving to truckers as they passed us at our slow rate of speed." He also remembered trips to Yellowstone Park and the Grand Canyon, as well as shorter trips to fishing spots in the Sierras. His family would travel to Jedediah Smith State Park to camp for a week at a time among the redwoods.

I was fortunate enough to be able to interview Jack at some length in 2009. Then eight-one, he was recovering from a broken hip suffered in a fall, and seemed distracted and in some pain, so the interview was not as long as I'd wished, but he told me enough to give me a picture of a family that used the bus extensively during his years of ownership. His most memorable trip was going across Colorado's Trail Ridge Road, the highest continuous paved highway in the United States. He also remembered visiting Pike's Peak: "Because we had gears, we'd gear it down on the way down, and subsequently, when the Highway Patrol would check people's brakes on the bottom, ours were still cool, so they'd let us keep on going." He remembered the trips that Marc would later write about, although it wasn't clear whether he was confusing their trips in the bus with others in the station wagon that they owned before that. The destinations rolled off his tongue ... the Grand Tetons, Yellowstone, Vail. "Casper and Cody in Wyoming. The caves in Oregon, Smith River, Crescent City, primarily Jedediah Smith State Park." He recalled vacations to Bishop and Bridgeport, Mammoth, June Lake, Mono Lake, and Convict Lake.

He remembered very few mechanical breakdowns, which he attributed to his habit of never exceeding fifty-five miles an hour. "No trouble. Once in a while ... we had an undersized starter, and when the battery got low once in a while, we had to give it a little push to start it. It would always start, so we'd park it on a hill under those conditions. We tried to keep a good battery in it." It had a good battery in it when he sold it, he told me. I didn't have the heart to tell him that that battery failed me on my first trip in the bus, and had to be replaced in Tulare. Of course, every battery is a good battery until it goes bad, and seldom does it give much warning before it fails.

I asked him if he could estimate how many miles he put on the bus, but he declined to do so. He remembered having to rebuild the engine at some point. "I actually took the engine out, took everything off it, did a complete rebuild ... new cylinders, everything so it had a new engine when you got it. That was about a year before you bought it. And the transmission had a little trouble in first gear, so I sent it over to AAMCO and they sent for a part or something. But instead they had a brand new transmission, still in the crate, so they gave me a brand new transmission and new clutch plate. They resurfaced the brakes, so it was in prime condition when you brought it."

I asked him about the oil cooler that it was equipped with. (As I've told elsewhere in this book, there's a great deal of controversy about whether these add-ons are beneficial or detrimental.) Jack came down firmly on the side of "beneficial." "The oil cooler, that was a definite purpose, and it had an extra quart of oil, which kept it running cooler. I didn't drive it over 55, didn't put a strain on things. I kept the air filter and features that went with it."

Something was wrong here. The bus didn't have the original air filter when I bought it, but one designed for a VW Beetle. I let it pass. Another Beetle part was the distributor, and I asked him about it. "When I was on a trip, it developed troubles, and I bought a new one. They told me that it would fit a bus."

We talked on for a little while longer, chatting about the various instruments he'd installed, and the custom-fitted carpeting and drapes he'd added. "I put carpeting in it, and you probably noticed that it was fitted and bound and it was pretty nice. Dark brown, so it didn't show problems with the food stains and things. And the ice box, I put a little better closure on it." He also installed two foot-rests for the driver, the left one to support the left leg in comfort and the right one, next to the throttle pedal, at such a height that one could keep his the pedal depressed exactly enough to produce a driving speed of between fifty-five and sixty on level ground.

He repainted the bus himself, changing it from all-white to the sand-and-white color scheme it now sports. He bought the paint in Santa Monica and applied it with a spray gun. "It was supposed to be good for maintenance; you didn't even have to put wax on it." He also removed the VW emblem from the front because it interfered with the bike rack he'd installed there, catching on the pedals of the bikes.

Jack never bought into the notion of keeping a car in stock condition. Like most owners, he saw the car as a work in progress, and never hesitated to customize it to his needs. In fact, I would do the same, although I would make a half-hearted attempt to make my modifications at least appear to be stock. But we weren't that different, he and I. He may not have approved of my returning the hubcaps to stock or restoring the bus's original oil-cooling system, but he would have no quarrel with my fixing the fuel gauge and the hand pump on the water tank, or with the roof racks I'd installed or the curtains I'd replaced, or with the power sockets and lights I'd installed to make camping easier. As for the spare tire, now mounted on the front, I didn't think he would object too much, despite the horror with which most restorers regard that practice.

He summarized his philosophy for me: "If you just keep the general plans that are set in motion with it, why, it's a nice item. Don't try to set it up for one of these resales...a lot of people will pay a premium price for one that old, 'cause they remember their earlier times and they have a lot of money and are willing to pay a premium. You can set it for yourself, so I say 'stick with it' and do it the way you want it. It's quite adaptable."

We got to the inevitable question: what prompted him to sell the bus? His voice got a little quieter. "Well, I had to get the driveway cleared, and it had set there for a long, long time, and Marc and I decided that it would be a long time before I get to go camping and things like that. So if I have a need, I can rent a camper or something, when and if that comes around. The hip was the problem." He reminded me of my father who, even after a devastating stroke had destroyed much of his vision and mobility, still retained some hope of getting back behind the wheel of his car. Maybe Jack would recover enough for one more trip. I hoped so.

"It broke my heart to sell George for Dad," Marc's letter concluded. "The saving grace is knowing that he is your hands and lives on. Dad thought of himself as master mechanic, but I fear that as money was always an issue, he tended to make do, as you can plainly see when you got him."

As I read this, I sincerely hoped that Jack's faith in me wasn't misplaced. I would do what I can to keep George on the road, in spite of my own limitations as a mechanic.

The Rehab Begins

Now that George was home, I was confronted with the same problem that every auto rebuilder faces: whether to bring it back as closely as possible to the way it was when it rolled off the production line in Hamburg, or to make compromises for the sake of comfort, lower expense, or practicality.

For the die-hard auto restorer, this is not an issue at all. There should be no compromises whatsoever. Everything should be as close to stock as it is humanly possible to make it. Any additions, any substitutions, any deviations at all from the original blueprints are Bad Things. The ultimate goal is to deliver a car that, should it suddenly travel back through time to the dealer's show-room, would be absolutely indistinguishable from any other model on the floor.

In his book *Standard Guide to Automotive Restoration*, Matt Joseph writes:

> "Inevitably, when the purpose(s) for undertaking a restoration are squared with the possibilities for restoration, a series of compromises results. These are compromises between some perfect ideal and some affordable, practical reality. Yet, having said that there must be compromises between the ideal, perfect duplication of original condition and some possible, achievable reality, I would quickly add that the ideal is easily stated and should never be very far from work that is actually done.
>
> "*The ideal is to authentically preserve and maintain, and to improve* [his italics]. This ideal can and should become an obsession for every restorer. No action should ever violate it. Temporary fixes have their place, but there is no place for damage."

But is this true for George? If it is, I'm already screwed. That Dormobile top was never original equipment for a 1971 Westfalia. I'd have to remove it and either rebuild the roof as it originally was, with the interior headliner, or possibly graft on a

Westfalia roof, which is available at some expense. Alternately, I could scrap the Westfalia interior and re-fit the bus with the genuine kit of the Dormobile company, for which absolutely no sources exist outside the United Kingdom (and precious little even there). Since I hadn't had a reply from the letter or email I sent that company, and since the only supplier of Dormobile roof parts that I could locate refused to ship out of the UK, this course of action seems doomed from the start.

I realized that restoration wasn't my goal, although I had used the word elsewhere as shorthand to explain to my non-car friends what I was doing. I realized that I was sailing under false colors, but my intent wasn't to deceive but to save myself from lengthy explanations. There was, in fact, a better word for what I'm doing: rehabilitation. What I was restoring was not George's original look or its equipment, but its original purpose, which is to travel around and be camped in. Once it was a perfectly functional camper, and it would be again. But it would be improved in several respects. First, it would have better tires than the ones that came with the bus. It would have a better sound system, one capable of plugging my iPod into, as well as upgraded speakers (although not as elaborate as the multi-speaker system that Jack installed, with its rat's nest of wiring). It would have more cabinet space, and brighter lights.

The art of rehabilitating a camper is not too far different from repairing a musical instrument like a guitar. If the soundboard is damaged beyond repair, the luthier has a choice of replacing it with another one with acoustic properties as identical as possible to the original, taking detailed notes, and saving the original pieces along with the restored instrument. The new piece will be glued in with hot hide glue, both to match the glue already in the guitar and to make the repair "reversible" if necessary, since hide glue will come apart when heated to around 140° Fahrenheit. For an instrument that will be returned to a museum, this is the only responsible course of action.

But let's say that the owner wants to keep playing the instrument, with a hard playing style will ask a lot more of the guitar than it was originally designed to take, and with a tone that the original didn't have. In addition, she also points out that the reason the original soundboard failed was because it wasn't properly braced on the inside. Our luthier is now confronted with a different set of choices. To satisfy the customer, he might choose a wood with different acoustic properties and tonalities. He may also take the opportunity to brace it differently, correcting the original flaw in the bracing design. He may also choose to use a different finish or a different glue, taking advantage of technological improvements that have been made in the thirty years since the guitar was originally built. The result is a guitar that has been ruined from a conservation standpoint, because it no longer resembles the instrument that it was before. But, if the luthier knows his stuff, it may be a better-sounding, longer-lasting, and more functional guitar than it was before.

In the months to come, the process of returning George to the road would continue to pose the restore/rehabilitate dilemma. Restoring it to factory specifications would have been beyond my present budget, and wouldn't have given me the practical camper I wanted. It pleased me to get rid of the more unsightly modifications it had accumulated through the years, but what I wanted in the end was a reliable, comfortable vehicle that was my personal vision of what an ideal camper should be. It would have the classic lines, as far as possible, but I was willing to make some compromises in favor of safety and functionality that a purist wouldn't. And it was with this goal in mind that I began George's rehabilitation.

In Sacramento, there's a garage called Kombi Haus, owned by a young man named Justin Campbell. It specializes in air-cooled Volkswagens, although it will work on other cars if asked to by their loyal customers, most of whom wouldn't dream of taking their cars anywhere else. But Justin prefers to describe his services as "VW repair and restoration" and advertises it that way. Justin is tall and blond, with Buddy Holly glasses and a grin that shows a lot of teeth. In a way, he seems too young to know his business, since he loves to work on cars that were built before he was born, but a short conversation with him convinced me that he'd seen just about everything that can go wrong with an air-cooled vehicle. He takes the concept of restoration very seriously, preferring where possible to return a vehicle to stock configuration whenever possible. When his garage repaints a car (and he has full facilities to do so) he will research what colors the car originally came in and will recommend that you repaint it the same way, or with a color scheme that was available for that car and year.

He also collects antique bicycles, and has a few dozen of them hanging from the rafters of the shop. Two blocks away, he has a second shop for the auto body and painting, and the bicycles are used to go back and forth between the two. (This reminded me of when Pacific Airwave operated, for a while, between two buildings across the street from each other, and scooters and skateboards were used for the same purpose.) At VW shows, he sometimes brings an old penny-farthing and offers opportunities to ride it.

For a hundred dollars, Kombi Haus will inspect a car and give you a rundown on what needs fixing now, what needs fixing eventually, and what it will all cost. It's a good investment; for one thing, they can put it on a lift and get a much better view of the underneath of the car than your average shade-tree mechanic could have.

So on Monday, July 14, 2008, I drove the bus to Kombi Haus, throwing my bicycle in the back so I could leave it with them, pedal the mile and a half back to my house, do the books for the tent-making business I had, and wait for their call. The call came at about two o'clock.

Justin and his staff had given the bus a thorough going-over, and found a lot of stuff wrong with it. Most of it was due to age; things like the brake lines, shocks, voltage regulator, plugs, wires, and ignition coil were all old or at the end of their wear cycle and would need to be replaced. The vacuum advance on the distributor was faulty, and Justin recommended that I replace it with a centrifugal-advance distributor. The exhaust system would need to be replaced by and by. The oil light flickered at low idle speeds (something I hadn't noticed before, although I should have), signifying either a weak oil pump or wear inside the engine bearings, or possibly an obstruction in the hoses going to and from the external oil cooler.

Justin didn't like the oil cooler. Although properly installed oil coolers did cool the engine down by twenty degrees or so, there was much that could go wrong with them. I asked him if it would make more sense just to take the damn thing off and replace it with the stock oil cooler. He agreed that the result would probably be more trouble-free, and that if I paid attention to the engine and didn't over-tax it, I could probably get by just fine with the stock cooler. He did recommend that I retain the oil filter, since it added a little oil capacity to the engine and did a better job of filtering crud out than the wire screen in the sump.

He also didn't like the air cleaner. It was from a bug, not a bus, and was held up by that weird little scaffold I mentioned earlier. When I asked him if it would be wise to replace the oil-bath cleaner with a paper-element cleaner, he said that it would be better to use the stock oil-bath air cleaner that came with the bus.

Well, all of what he said made sense. It would cost a lot of money in parts, but I had done every one of those procedures on my earlier buses, and didn't feel that any of it was outside my zone of competence. I could do them a weekend at a time, over the course of the winter. But the bodywork was something else again ...

I had entertained a notion of doing the bodywork myself as well, by enrolling in a vocational school class on that subject. After all, the schools allowed their students to work on their own cars, and the tuition wouldn't be anything close to the $2400 that Justin thought the labor would come to. (I'd still have to pay for the parts, though, and that would come to about $1100 right there.) I could learn bodywork, and add the story of that education to the book I was writing. What a great idea!

But as I listened to Justin describing the bodywork that needed to be done, I had second thoughts. The job was a lot more intricate than I had imagined, the damage more extensive, the skills more demanding. I began to doubt that I could learn enough about the specific skills to do the job the way it needed to be done. If I have learned anything about buses over forty-five years, it is that they are put together differently from American iron, and there was every reason to think that the repair procedures would be similarly unique to that breed. Why not let the experts do their work? That way, there would be no doubt that it had been done right, and the resale value of the bus would be enhanced. That $2400 was starting to sound like money well spent.

I had been right that the right rear quarter-panel would be the biggest problem. The area formerly occupied by the scoops on both sides would have to be replaced entirely, since there was no good way to patch them without exposing a seam. Not only that, but the battery tray on the right side (the floor on which the battery itself sits) would also have to be completely reconstructed, and the air cooler pedestal replaced. New lights and lenses would be installed to replace the ones that had either broken or been replaced by non-stock parts.

The windshield also turned out to be just the sort of horror show I had dreaded. It was impossible to determine just how far the rust extended underneath the windshield seal. That wouldn't be known for sure until the windshield itself had been removed, along with the metal that held it in place. With luck, the rust wouldn't extend into the area of the lower portion of the front panel, or affect the mounting of the dashboard.

No doubt about it. My $4000 bus would end up being a $10,000 bus before the year was out, what with the bodywork, parts, and a new paint job. For that kind of money, I could have bought another bus in better condition. But I recognized that I was starting to lose my perspective and ability to think rationally. George was starting to get under my skin. I was falling prey to the most deadly affliction that can beset the vintage-car buff: the dream of rescuing a fading beauty, restoring it, and giving it back to the world. I would have the same relationship to this bus that I had to my other three, a relationship based on being acquainted with every wire terminal, every grease fitting, every sheet-metal screw, and every bulb. I had lost my previous three buses to rust and the infirmities of age. Perhaps I can reverse the trend with this one.

There was one important difference between this bus and its predecessors: it would not be my main source of transportation. For that, I had the Sienna. This would allow me to take a little

105

more time with the things that needed it, without having to put it back on the road in the shortest time possible. For the first time, I would be doing a procedure at a time of my own choosing, not because I had to get the car back on the road right away. I had never had this luxury before, and was going to count on it to help me do the best possible job.

I'd planned on going on a business trip which would last a month, so it seemed like as good a time as any to let Kombi Haus have the bus to replace the rear quarter panels. After groping around inside the engine compartment, I discovered that the original stock oil cooler was missing, and that the fan housing that accommodated it had been replaced somewhere down the line with one that didn't. Or perhaps it was the original fan housing, but modified so that the chamber that originally housed the oil cooler had been cut away. So it looked like the fan housing itself would have to be replaced, as well. Justin told me that it looked like the engine would have to come out anyway, so that the repairs to the body could be done. If that was the case, it was probably the best time to retrofit everything back to stock, even though it would add considerably to the cost of the job. If I wanted to retain the oil filter, extra holes would have to be bored into the case to shunt the oil circulation from the galleries cast into the block, and divert it into a separate circuit that the oil filter could use. And that, of course, meant even more money.

The only other upside to having the engine out was that it made it easier to have the fuel tank removed and de-sludged, and to trouble-shoot (and replace, if necessary) the fuel gauge sending unit.

But the bodywork would come first, so I drove the bus over to the Kombi Haus and gave Justin a thousand-dollar down payment.

When I got back from my business trip a month later, I had a roaring cold. But I wanted to see how George was doing. As it turns out, the folks at Kombi Haus had never received the email I sent giving them permission to return the oil cooler to its stock configuration, and they had let that be for the moment. They'd already repaired the two rear quarter-panels.

Justin and I walked a block to their new body shop, recently vacated by Precision Auto Body, who had moved to larger quarters a mile or so south of Kombi Haus. George was the only car there, and sat inside the spray booth. The bodywork looked good, but it only made the front of the car look worse. "In for a penny, in for a pound," I thought, and decided to get the windshield area repaired, as well. Justin said that it would cost about a grand to get the windshield removed and the damaged portions of the front removed, a new piece welded in, the windshield replaced, and the bare metal repainted with primer. The estimate also included a new windshield. We might as well do it now, Justin said, since most of the cost of a windshield replacement is labor and seals, and all that money will have to be spent anyway. He added that we really wouldn't know the condition of the metalwork behind the front panel until the outside was peeled away. If the rust had affected the interior panel, that too would have to be replaced or repaired. But I was optimistic that if rust was indeed there, it would be minor.

A week later, I was feeling much better. I went back to Kombi Haus, gave permission for the work to be done on the front of the bus, and paid Justin another two thousand dollars.

On September 2, at eight-thirty in the morning, the phone rang. It was Justin. "I have some bad news," he said. It turned out that the rust damage was a lot more extensive than I'd thought. It extended into the panel that sits behind the front panel, and affected the vent system as well. The price had gone up at least five hundred dollars. I told him to wait until I could come over and see the damage for myself. It wouldn't make much difference, though, I reflected. The work would have to be done, sooner or later. I was also thankful, suddenly, that I decided not to do the bodywork myself; I would have found myself in over my head, and probably would have ended up taking the job to Kombi Haus anyway.

At one in the afternoon, I was looking at the damage, and it was as bad as Justin said it was. With a tool resembling a bent, dull screwdriver, he poked holes through the front panel at will. There was nothing but rust there. If he pushed through the outer layer, the tool would hit the inner wall, and go through that one, too. Both layers would have to be replaced, down to the area where the fresh-air vents were located. So I approved another six hundred dollars' worth of work to be done. Justin said that this sort of rust damage was fairly common, particularly with buses that have been parked in coastal areas. If Jack, the bus's previous owner, had been more on top of things, he could have seen this damage and nipped it in the bud, but he didn't. It was a costly mistake, on my part rather than his, because I was the one who was going to have to foot the bill for fixing it.

Two days later, I was passing the Kombi Haus's new body shop on another errand, and saw Justin standing outside. He was waiting for a VW bus to arrive from Vacaville on a trailer and, as I parked my Sienna, it pulled up. "1969?" I asked, displaying my intimate knowledge of bay-window buses. I was wrong, of course. It was a 1968. The giveaway was the configuration of the front door handles, which I missed. 1968 was the only year that particular configuration was used on a bay window bus, which makes those parts fairly scarce.

While I was there, Justin showed me the "cut-in clip" for my bus. It was in pretty good shape, only a little surface rust, and was painted the ugly chartreuse that many of the buses of that era sported. It had a tire carrier already attached to it, and showed the dimples in the metalwork typically caused when you attach a tire to a front of the bus (one reason why Justin dislikes them). He would pound out as much of the damage as he could, but would keep the tire carrier on the panel. He also pointed out some rust on the rear hatch and showed me another one he had, which he would sell me for $80.00.

As Justin regarded the clip, he turned philosophical. "Some bus had to die, so that others can live."

I noticed a mid-sixties bus in the lot with a Dormobile top like mine. It turned out to be one of Justin's own buses. The interior was also Westfalia, so it must have been a similar conversion. The top was in pretty good shape, but the interior had seen better days.

Two weeks and over six thousand dollars later, all the major bodywork was finished and the bus was sitting in my driveway again, ready for the next round of expenditures. The day before, I had watched Damon and Jim install the new windshield. They worked smoothly as a team, lifting the glass into place. As Jim pushed on the windshield from the outside, Damon pulled out the cord that Jim had previously inserted into the channel in the weatherstrip where the flange on the perimeter of the windshield would fit. "Sometimes they don't go in that easily," Jim told me. "Sometimes we have to do it two or three times." I told him that it was a tribute to his skills in welding in all the new metal below the windshield. He said it's usually just variations in the glass itself that cause the problem.

I had been shopping for tires, and found that the type that fits the bus had gotten a lot rarer, and consequently more expensive, than they used to be. It's not the size alone, but the combination of size and construction, that makes them scarce. A bus weighs about a ton and a half when empty, but can carry roughly another ton in cargo, so its tires can expect to carry a load of about five thousand pounds. The tires currently on the bus, bought under emergency circumstances, in Castiac, had a load rating of only 1168 pounds, and the owners manual recommended a minimum rating of 1520 pounds. Not only that, but they were a couple of inches smaller in diameter than the recommended ones.

After getting the new tires installed, I drove to Pep Boys to pick up a few things for the bus. As I drove, it suddenly occurred to me that for the previous four hundred miles or so, I had actually been sitting about an inch closer to the road than I used to with Thunderbus. Now that I was back where I was supposed to be, I was amazed that I could actually detect that small difference in parallax. Everything felt exactly where it ought to be again.

The headliner of the '71 Westfalia camper is made of thin birch plywood, not fabric. When I bought the bus, that headliner had seen a lot of moisture and was starting to weaken and delaminate, resulting in some ugly sag and splintering. This plywood was not easy to come by, but eventually I found a source of it here in Sacramento, at a specialty hardwood company. I bought a 5' x 5' sheet, which bent very nicely to fit into the rear cargo area of my Sienna.

I removed the old headliner, laid it on top of the sheet of plywood, and traced its outline. I also marked the location of the various holes that were used to affix it to the frame of the bus, and of the dome light and its mounting plate. The headliner was in bad shape around the edges, but there was enough left to determine its original dimensions. I carefully cut it out with a saber saw, drilled and cut the appropriate holes, and gave it a couple of coats of a wipe-on polyurethane.

The new headliner went in without a hitch, once I figured out how it was originally installed. I took the opportunity to remove one of the folding cots, since it was damaged and I wouldn't use it anyway. I left the other one in for the moment, figuring that I could use it as an upper shelf for storage when I was camping. Eventually, the other cot was removed as well, resulting in my carrying about fifty pounds less.

(For the rest of this chapter, I'm going to simply quote from the journal I kept when doing the work. Thus the shift to present tense, because that's the way I wrote it, and it seems to read better that way. We pick up the action about a week after the headliner is replaced.)

September 19, 2008

It's a beautiful Friday afternoon, and I've been working on the bus. I adjust the valves, replace the valve cover gaskets, drain the oil, and clean the oil sump cover and screen. There's a lot of gunk there, which surprises me, since the oil filter should have been trapping most of that stuff. The next step is to adjust the points and timing.

When I get the engine running, I open the engine compartment and find, to my horror, that there's a leak from the high-voltage terminal of the coil to the plus side, resulting in a series of bright blue sparks leaping the gap, inches away from the fuel line and fuel filter. Not good at all.

So I call Justin and order a new coil and a set of spark plug wires as well, since the problem could be caused by a failure in the wire that goes from the coil to the distributor cap.

110

I install the coil and spark plug wires, but still can't get it running right, so I take the bus back to Kombi Haus and leave it there. The word comes back that I've mixed up two of the spark plug leads, causing two cylinders to misfire. (Yesterday was not one of my better mechanicking days.) But they also tell me that the carburetor has failed, and ask me to approve a replacement. I figure I'm getting a rebuilt Solex 34PICT-3, so I agree.

When I get the bus back, what's sitting on top of the intake manifold is not a rebuilt Solex but a new Brosol H30/31 carburetor, a Brazilian-made carburetor designed to replace a large number of Solex carburetors. I am assured by the Kombi Haus people that the rebuilt 34PICT-3s are pretty much unobtainable, and that they've had better luck with the Brosols than with the rebuilts they've acquired recently.

And the carburetor wasn't the only problem. They tell me that the distributor has developed a vacuum leak in that part of the mechanism that determines how much the timing advances during acceleration.

(After checking parts numbers, I find that my distributor is not the one that came with the bus but was made for a Bug. Like the original, it uses both a vacuum-advance and a vacuum-retard mechanism to match the 34PICT-3 carburetor; this combination was evidently what VW needed to pass California's smog standards at the time.)

I go back to the Internet to learn about the Brosol carburetor. It seems to have a solid reputation, although some have complained that their models developed leaks and wear at only five thousand miles or so of operation. Others claim that Brosol's quality control has improved mightily in recent years, and that the new ones can be relied on. I decide to keep this one and give it a try.

So what do I use for a distributor? Justin recommends a Bosch 009 distributor, a non-vacuum mechanical advance distributor. Although Bosch stopped making them, there are several versions of the "009-type" distributor from a number of sources. They range from fairly cheap to horrendously expensive. Back to the computer I go.

If I thought that the Solex/Brosol controversy was hot, I wasn't prepared for the religious wars conducted between those who favored the 009 distributor and those who despised it. As I follow the conversations on the more popular forums, I read that the 009 was originally developed as a distributor for static engines, which didn't need sophisticated timing-advance mechanisms. It advanced the timing through weights that rotated the interior plate that the points were mounted on; as the distributor's rotation increased with engine speed, the weights were forced out through centrifugal force. As long as the restraining springs didn't break, the mechanism was robust and reliable.

Later, the 009 became favored by the racing community, another bunch that didn't have to deal with much stop-and-go traffic. Since their engines were going flat out most of the time, they didn't need anything more complex than a simple advance mechanism. Meanwhile, VW was fitting its engines with distributors that were actuated not by centrifugal force but by the vacuum the engine was producing. In many ways, this was the more intelligent approach, because vacuum increased as the throttle plate was opened, and this was precisely when the timing needed to be advanced. The increased vacuum moved a diaphragm to which a small rod was connected, rotating the points plate proportionately. The drawback was that when the diaphragm in the distributor developed a leak and failed, there was no advance at all, and the engine couldn't cope with variations in engine speed. Later on, VW used a combination of the two, so that a vacuum failure would be inconvenient but not catastrophic.

The popularity of the 009 got a big boost when John Muir wholeheartedly recommended them as replacements for the stock distributor. His evangelism resulted in thousands of them being sold. And, in fact, they worked well with most of the carburetors supplied for the bug and bus up until the late sixties, when VW began tweaking them for minimum emissions. These new carburetors didn't work as well with the straight centrifugal-advance distributors, and many drivers noticed a sort of "flat spot" in the advance curve, where an accelerated engine

112

seemed to falter and lose power before the advance kicked in. People also reported higher engine temperatures and lower gas mileage. Probably the worst carburetor to use a 009 with was the 34PICT-3, which was designed for the dual-vacuum advance to the exclusion of other forms. (It was also the carburetor I had on the Thunder Bus when I fitted it out with the 009 on Muir's recommendation. That may well have been the reason I was getting only forty thousand miles on a pair of heads.) Gradually, the 009 lost favor with the multitudes, and it became the fashion to put them down at every opportunity.

Now that I need to find a new distributor, I look for suggestions. Like the 34PICT-3 carburetor, my distributor does not seem to be readily available as a rebuilt. Instead, most people recommend what is known as a SVDA (single vacuum, dual advance) distributor. This beast used both a vacuum mechanism and a spring mechanism to advance the timing. VW provided them as stock with some Beetles and buses of the late sixties, and there are a few high-end companies that rebuild them specifically for use with the carbs of that that era. But only the most expensive of these were reputed to work well with the Brosol carburetor.

My problem is compounded by the same fact that haunts every driver of a car whose original parts are no longer available: once you start using non-original parts with different performance specifications, you find they don't play well with other parts. This leads you to consider using other non-original parts that might work better with the new part. When it comes to finding out how to get these parts to operate harmoniously with each other, the factory manuals are no longer of much help. You've got figure that out on your own, or hope that somebody else somewhere has tried the same combination you have, and has written up the results for others to share.

One of my Internet buddies, who goes by the online name of "Static," tells me that he got good advice, good parts, and good service from a Texan named Keith Doncaster. It was Keith who told him to discard that 009 in favor of a vacuum-advance distributor. Keith's mission in life is to rebuild distributors and carburetors, and sell them to bus mavens at reasonable prices.

His reputation in the VW community is as solid as they come. It seems that I need Keith's advice, too, so I email him.

Keith promptly replies, although he's got his hands full at the moment; he's cleaning the debris left by Hurricane Ike. It will be a while before his shop is ready, he says, but if I email him about what I've got and what I need, he'll see what he can do. I send it off that night, and the next day he asks me to give him a call.

His recommendation surprises me. He says that the best thing for my bus is ... the 009 distributor. It works well with the Brosol carbs, he says, and he would trust it over any rebuilt vacuum distributor, even his own. Like many people, he doesn't think that the vacuum supplied by the Brosol carb is strong enough to power most of the less expensive SVDA distributors on the market. The dreaded "flat spot" problem is hardly noticeable, he says, and if I've driven any amount with a 34PICT-3 and a centrifugal-advance distributor (I have), I probably learned long ago how to compensate for it. He has a newly-rebuilt Bosch German-made 009 – the highest quality around – that he can let me have for fifty dollars, including new points and condensor and test-spun on his bench. If I don't like it, I can send it back to him and he'll rebuild me a vacuum-advance distributor, at some extra cost.

I'm sold. I send him a check, and the 009 arrives in the mail a few days later. I install it this morning, time it (the dwell is already right on) and drive to the bank. The engine purrs like a kitten. I also buy some bolts to put the new tire carrier on the front. This afternoon, the UPS driver shows up with a box containing four new hub-caps and a tire cover. At long last, George is starting to look and sound like a proper bus again.

Before I go on a business trip, I call my friend Tom to help me troubleshoot the looseness in the front end. Tom's no mechanic, but he doesn't need to be; his job is to sit in the front seat and either move the steering wheel or hold it steady when I tell him to. The only problem I find is a little looseness in the right front wheel bearing, which I tighten. A road test tells me that most, but not all, of the slop in the steering is now gone.

While I'm away on a trip, a package arrives. It's the new distributor cap and rotor I ordered from a parts dealer, along with a radio antenna and some new front shock absorbers. I install the new antenna and the shocks. While I'm under the bus, I tighten up the steering box a tad, lube the front torsion bars and swing lever bushing, and check the fluid level in the steering box and transmission. I also take the time to check the apparatus for hooking the bus up to household electrical power, which consists of a box on the outside to which an extension cord can be connected and a pair of receptacles on the inside of the bus. Amazingly, everything works. It may be the first system I've checked in the bus that hasn't needed further attention.

A few days later, I've decided that the limited adjustment I had made to the steering box wasn't enough to make for secure driving, so I take the bus to the Kombi Haus. I know that there's some sort of internal adjustment that can be made to the steering box, and that it means disassembling it, a process so involved that John Muir never wrote up a procedure for it; he felt that it was beyond the capacities of the everyday mechanic and suggested that Volkswagen take care of it. Unfortunately, nobody at Volkswagen dealerships today even knows what you're talking about.

It turns out that Kombi Haus doesn't do the procedure, either. But they identified some dry ball joints and worn tie rods that might have contributed to the problem, and replaced them. It wasn't cheap, and it didn't really solve the problem (although it reduced it somewhat). But I knew that the work had to be done eventually, so I didn't feel too bad about laying out the money. It looks like I'll have to find a used steering box by and by, and have it rebuilt to original specifications.

November 26, 2008

The time has arrived to fix the fuel gauge. As I mentioned earlier, my first bus didn't even have one, but every subsequent vehicle I've owned did, and it's one of those things that one becomes accustomed to. The fact that Jack never bothered to fix it can only mean that he found the task beyond his abilities or finances; this should have been a warning to me of things to come.

I had already bought a used gas gauge and fuel gauge sender (a device installed in the gas tank which senses the amount of fuel in the tank and signals this information to the gas gauge). I figured that the problem had to be in one of these components or, possibly, in the electrical connection between them. The easiest component to get at was the fuel gauge, so I started with that.

I pulled the instrument cluster containing the gauge out of the dashboard. Tacked onto the back of the fuel gauge was a vibrator, usually used to stabilize the voltage and provide a more accurate reading. There was a mystery here: Volkswagen didn't start to use vibrators until 1972, so what was one doing on a '71 bus? It further appeared that the vibrator was home-made. I began to wonder if Jack had somehow replaced the original fuel gauge and sender with one for a later model, for reasons unknown.

Well, I knew that the used gas gauge I bought was good, so I installed it in the instrument cluster and turned on the power. No luck; the tank still read 5/8 full, even though I had calculated that there was less than half a tankful.

Well, that meant that it had to be either the sender or the wire. I knew where the wire connected to the gauge was, and to check its condition I needed to find the other end. It turns out that there is a connector that you were supposed to be able to access somewhere in the engine compartment, or in the area just underneath the floor of the fuel tank compartment (according to the write-ups that various people had posted on the Internet). But when I went looking for that connector, I couldn't find it at all. I would have to trace it back from the terminal on the sender itself. I imagined Jack had already performed all these steps, and began to appreciate why he might have given up at this point.

The sender, mounted in the fuel tank, cannot be reached until you take the fuel tank out, and you can't do that without removing the engine and an intervening bulkhead. This is a fairly

116

serious proposition for a weekend mechanic without garage equipment like floor jacks or lifts.

But it turns out to be unnecessary, if you are willing to cut a hole in a precisely determined place on the rear luggage deck of the bus, behind the passenger seat. VW restorers decry this practice, but as I have explained earlier, I was no longer interested in restoring the bus to show-room condition, but was just trying to make it a serviceable camper. And even VW had recommended this procedure and provided a small plate to cover the hole. That plate was no longer available as a replacement part, of course, but it was no great task to fabricate a substitute. I made the measurements, cut the hole, and exposed the sender.

Attached to the sender, of course, was the wire that eventually communicated with the gauge. I had pretty much decided that the problem was with the sender. After all, what can go wrong with a simple wire? But I got out my ohmmeter and checked the wire just the same.

Good thing I did. There was no continuity between the exposed terminal end of the wire and the corresponding wire in the gauge. In fact, there was no real evidence that the two terminals were ends of the same wire. But when I improvised a wire to run from the sender to the gauge and turned the key, the gauge dropped to half full. So it appeared that it had been the wire all along.

There was only one thing to be done. I had to run a new wire from the gauge to the sender, a distance of some fifteen feet. Of course, I couldn't simply sling the wire underneath the chassis of the bus, where it might be damaged. Instead, I had to remove the kick panel under the dash and another pan under the front of the car, thread the wire through the various access holes and frame members, secure the wires, and replace the kick panel and pan. Finally, I devised a plate to repair and seal the hole I had created in the rear luggage deck. (Instead of pop rivets, I used screws, against the odd chance that I, or some future owner, might need to replace the sending unit.)

After I drove to the gas station and put in 7.2 gallons, it read 7/8 full. The activity took the better part of two days, but I had a working gauge at the end, without having to resort to removing

117

the engine. Someday, when the engine is out, I'll see if I can trace the original wire to wherever it goes.

While I was spending all that time under the dashboard, I took the opportunity to remove some instruments installed by Jack in the past, including a tachometer (which had been working erratically) and an oil temperature gauge (which hasn't worked since the bus came back from the Kombi Haus in August), along with their associated wiring. It greatly simplified the rat's nest of wiring under the dash and the job of trouble-shooting the remaining circuits. In the process, I discovered a switch, also installed by Jack, that turned the dashboard clock on and off. It was in the "off" position. When I switchet it to "on" the clock starts ticking! A working clock on a bus this old is a rarity, so I was quite satisfied.

December 7, 2008

And I spoke too soon about the clock. It works intermittently, even though it seems to have current all the time. It probably needs to be taken out and given a good clean.

Now that the weather is colder, the sliding door was becoming much harder to open. The pivot arm at the rear of the door seemed to be hanging up, requiring me to grab at the underside of the door and pull hard before the door would open and slide rearward. I disassembled the door latch assembly, and the pivot arm was in perfect shape. Looking elsewhere for the problem, I eventually took the rear locking mechanism off and found that the grease had congealed to the texture of candle wax over the last thirty-eight years. I took it to Kombi Haus where Justin put it into their degreaser. When I got it back, I put in new lithium grease and reinstalled the mechanism, and now the door practically leaps open when I turn the handle.) Moral: Don't assume that a mechanical assembly has failed before you clean it off and lube it.

While I had the door off, I noted that the seal around the door was shot, and moisture had been coming in from underneath for some time now. Fortunately, it didn't cause any rusting, but the wooden panel covering the interior of the door had started to rot and delaminate. I have enough plywood left over from the headliner repair to replace it, but I don't want to attempt it until the door seal is replaced.

January 3, 2009

My oil temperature gauge has arrived from the Bus Depot, so I installed it this weekend. It required running yet another wire from the dashboard to the rear of the bus. (There was another wire that Jack McNeil used when he installed his oil temp gauge, but part of it had been damaged when the engine was taken out last August.) Once hooked up, I get an absurdly low reading – only a hundred degrees – but I'll trouble-shoot that later.

From another supplier, I receive a replacement seal for the sliding door. I take it down to the Kombi Haus, where Damon explains how it fits into the door (the original being too far deteriorated to give me useful information). It goes in easily, without the need of using glue. This is convenient, since it will have to come out again when I finally get the money to repaint the bus, at which time I will also have the remaining door and window seals replaced.

January 13, 2009

I'm getting ready for Buses By the Bridge, a huge bus show in Arizona. I tuned up the bus's engine today. The dwell, which I had set at 50° when I installed the 009 distributor, had drifted to 56° in the intervening months. So I reset it back to 50°, a job that ended up taking the better part of an hour. Unlike the distributors on most cars, the Bosch version does not allow you to set the dwell while the engine is running. Instead, you have to remove the distributor cap and rotor, rotate the engine until a lobe on the distributor shaft is in precise alignment with its corresponding nylon rider on the movable part of the points apparatus, and measure the gap between the points with a feeler gauge. If it's out of spec, you loosen a hold-down screw and pry the moveable plate an infinitesimal amount. Then you tighten the hold-down screw, replace the rotor and distributor cap, go to

119

the front of the car and start it up, go back to the engine compartment, attach the dwell-tachometer, and get a reading.

It will be off.

You sigh deeply, disconnect the dwell-tach, go to the front of the car and turn the engine off, and repeat the above procedure. Since the adjustment is so sensitive, it usually takes five or six attempts to get it right, and more if you do things like forgetting to replace the rotor after you adjust the points. With other distributors, you simply insert an allen wrench into an adjustment port and turn it back and forth, with the engine continually running, until you get the reading you want on the dwell-tach ... a process that takes maybe thirty seconds, tops.

Changing the dwell setting also changes the timing. So I got the timing light out and re-adjusted that, which is done by loosening the distributor clamp and rotating the distributor a minute amount this way or that, until the light lights up at the precise moment that a pre-set mark on the crankshaft pulley lines up with the joining seam of the crankcase when the pulley is rotated. This sets the "static" timing.

There's another method called "dynamic" timing, which you do with the engine running. With this method, you use a strobe light and another pre-set mark on the crankshaft pulley and see where the marks line up at various engine speeds. As the engine revolutions increase, certain gizmos like vacuum advance levers and springs actuate, and only with a strobe light can you see if these gizmos are doing their job. Arguably, this is a better way to time the engine, because it shows what the engine is doing at the speeds at which it actually operates. But the strobe light costs more, and a lot of VW gurus maintain that as long as the distributor is in good shape, a static timing light is easier and more foolproof to operate. (Ever the pragmatist, John Muir recommended that, if you doubt whether your timing marks on the crankshaft pulley are in the right place, you take the car to Volkswagen and have them time it with their equipment. When you get home, you take out your static timing light, put your own marks at the appropriate places on the pulley, and use those marks exclusively.)

I used both methods, since I had a timing light. As it turned out, the two methods resulted in readings that agreed fairly well, so I didn't worry much about it.

Then I did a compression check, the ultimate indicator of engine health. The results were satisfactory — one hundred forty pounds of pressure in all the cylinders except number three, which was ten pounds lower. (This is not uncommon in VW engines that have had some miles on them, since that cylinder gets less of the cooling air than the others do.) While I had the spark plugs out, I checked their gap (at 0.025 inches, right on spec) and their color (quite black, indicating that the engine was running rich). This was no surprise, since I hadn't been getting the gas mileage I was expecting. If readjusting the timing and dwell didn't improve my gas mileage, I'll probably take the bus back to Kombi Haus to have the carburetor fine-tuned.

I also checked the oil ... a quart low. Again, this is not unusual in worn engines, but it tells me that I'll need to keep an eye on this in the future, since a VW engine is as much oil-cooled as air-cooled, and this particular kind of coolant isn't provided in abundance from our atmosphere.

The tune-up done, I use the remaining daylight to install a borrowed CB radio. This required fashioning a bracket for it and bolting it to the underside of the dashboard, using a hole that Jack McNeil had drilled earlier for some unknown purpose.

Now the bus is as ready as I can make it for Buses By the Bridge. It may not be show quality, but it's now functional and trustworthy. The "shakedown cruises" of two campouts have proved their worth.

Or so I thought.

January 15, 2009

At one minute after six in the morning, I'm meeting Justin and his kids in front of the Kombi Haus. By 6:20, we're on Highway 99 heading toward Stockton to add Damon to our convoy.

Twenty miles down the road, I meet disaster. The exhaust volume increases mightily, the bus shakes and loses power. It

121

sounds like a burned valve to me. Justin is in front of me, but he doesn't see me flashing my headlights wildly as I pull over to the side of the road.

Naturally, I've just passed an exit, so I have to cross the Consumnes River and take the next exit at Dillard Road. From there, I pull off the road and call Justin on the cell phone (he wasn't able to get his CB radio repaired, so mine was useless). I describe the trouble and wish him Godspeed. It's now 6:45 or so. So far today, I've experienced anticipation, wanderlust, shock, and despair, and the sun isn't even up yet.

The engine is severely ill, but I'm able to limp back into Sacramento on my own power (or three-quarters of my own power). No tow truck for me this time — it's a matter of pride. I park it in the back yard, go inside, and make two more cups of coffee. At this point I could call it off, or I could scramble to find another engine to put into the bus (since I really don't have the time to dismantle the present one). Or I could take the Sienna. I've camped in it before. It wasn't nearly as comfortable as the Westie, but it could be done. I really don't want to miss Buses by the Bridge, and my better angels persuade me that getting a new engine is a bad idea for two reasons: the cost of a complete turn-key engine would be prohibitive, and it would be folly to road-test a brand-new engine on a thousand-mile trip unless it was absolutely necessary.

So I end up taking the Sienna to Buses By the Bridge. *[Author's note: that trip is described elsewhere in this book.]*

January 20, 2009

When I get home, I push the bus into the back yard and, using a tiny floor jack I bought at Kragen, I remove the engine from the bus. As I'm dismantling all the tin, I notice something sticking out of the head at the spark plug socket for the number one cylinder. It has the spark plug for that cylinder sticking out of it. It looks like some sort of spark plug extender, and I wonder why a previous owner might have installed it. The gadget has a great big hole in its side, and spark plug that's screwed into it is similarly damaged.

122

I make a few calls and pose the question on one of the VW forums, and the truth comes out. I installed it myself, by mistake. The "spark plug extender" turns out to be a fitting that came with the compression tester. It had been mounted on the end of the tester hose and I mistook it for part of the hose itself. After getting the compression reading, I unscrewed the hose, but I left the fitting still threaded into the head. (If I had had a few more brain cells firing, I might have noticed that the hose was a couple of inches shorter than when I had screwed it into the head. I might also have noticed that the spark plug was sitting out the same extra distance from the head when I replaced it.) And of course it was in the #1 spark plug hole, because that's the first cylinder you check when you do a compression test. (A few months later, Damon would find a similar fitting inside somebody else's engine. When he told me about it, I felt a little better about it.)

So there was never a burned valve after all. When the fitting finally failed, its hole zeroed the compression in the cylinder and sounded for all the world like a burned valve, but it appeared as if the engine itself had never sustained any damage. Just to be sure, I took the heads off, since I was 90% there anyway, and I thought that this was as good a time as any to fix a leaking push rod tube on the opposite side of the engine. An inspection of the heads revealed a few nascent cracks in the classic places that cracks develop in a dual-port heads, indicating that the heads were starting to show their age and would need to be replaced by and by.

Further inspection reveals something else. There are eight push rods in a VW engine, one for each valve. They are supposed to be exactly the same. However, as I'm cleaning the push rods prior to re-installing them, I notice that they seem to vary in thickness. I get out a caliper and a ruler and it turns out that they varied in length, too; I had three different kinds of pushrods in the engine. This is disquieting news. The only reason for the discrepancy is careless assembly. It appears that the last person who overhauled this engine used whatever parts he had lying around, and I'm not sure I want to trust it to any great extent.

And there's that flickering oil pressure light I mentioned a while earlier, which indicated a weak oil pump or worn bearings, both signs of an engine near the end of its wear cycle. It became obvious that when Jack had the engine "rebuilt," his mechanic replaced only the heads (and with inferior aftermarket ones, at that) and didn't open the crankcase to replace the main crankshaft bearings. While I might be able to put this engine back together and get a few thousand more miles out of it, it would be much better for me to replace it with one that I can trust not to fail on me for a while.

So I go to Kombi Haus. After the "spark plug extender" is passed around, provoking much hilarity and teasing, Justin looks at the heads and agrees that while I might be able to re-install them and use them for a while, there's not a whole lot of life left in them. He also approves of my decision to buy a new engine, particularly since his shop will be the one building it. One of his employees, a quiet man named Jim Bass, has been building engines for both racing and stock vehicles for some time, and he has an excellent reputation. Jim's manner is low-key, even diffident, but he has a reputation for meticulous work. When you say "Good morning" to him, he hesitates a second before answering, and you get the feeling that he's mentally checking the time to verify that it's still morning. That's the kind of guy you want building your engine. When he answers a question, it's more like he's offering suggestions than answers, but this allows you to feel free to follow up that question with more questions, so he can get a better bead on the questions you really should be asking.

Justin and I talk about what sort of engine would be best for the bus. For reliability, he recommends sticking with the stock 1600 dual-port that came with the bus, but also recommends the addition of a full-flow oil filter, since the bus engine doesn't come with one. I agree, since I had one on the Thunder Bus and never had to worry about oil contamination. We agree on a cost of about $1800 for the modified engine, a sizable chunk of money but worth it for my peace of mind, if I'm going to be doing as much traveling with this bus as I plan to. And it doesn't include a core charge for the old engine (which he doesn't want anyway). This gives me the option of rebuilding that engine at some point in the future, or selling it as a working engine for somebody who needs one cheap. I pay Justin half the amount as a deposit. The new engine will be available in three weeks, at which time I have to cough up the balance of the money.

February 4, 2009

It's been a couple of weeks since my last entry, and a lot has happened. George is now back on the road.

After commissioning the new engine, I reassembled the old one, using the old heads but putting new gaskets on whatever was taken apart. I also noticed that somebody had shortened a great deal of the lower part of each of the two intake manifolds, presumably to make them easier to install. This evidently caused some vacuum leakage in the past, because liberal amounts of sealant had been provided around the area where it mated with the boot that connected the lower part to the upper part of the manifold. One of the pieces was still serviceable, so I took the other one to Kombi Haus, and Charley located an identical part in the used part bin that hadn't been modified. I also put new boots on. Otherwise, I used all the old parts without giving them more than a brief clean.

I reinstalled the engine, and the process was fairly painless. Once the engine was in, it fired up without complaint, and I felt a measure of my self-confidence returning. Of course, I hadn't really done anything fundamental to it.

The next step was a road test, and it happened that some friends had planned a campout at Rio Vista, on the Sacramento River near the mouth of the Delta. I looked at the map and saw that State Route 160 wound gently along the bank of the river. It was a two-lane road and I figured that it wouldn't be heavily traveled, since Interstate 5 paralleled it only a few miles away. It appeared to be the perfect road for a test-drive.

Well, it wasn't. In fact, it turned out to be a levee road, many miles long with absolutely no place to pull off in the event of a breakdown for most of its length. But luck was finally with me, and the bus hummed along without a problem. I arrived at Rio

Vista, spent two nights there with the gang, and returned to Sacramento via the interstate I had shunned on the way down.

A New Heart

At the end of May, I decided that it was time to get back to work on the bus. The old engine came out again and I stripped it of all its peripherals, stopping only when I had removed all the tin from the long block. I had already bought the oil filter bracket (used, about five dollars) and the two hoses (very new and expensive, about fifty dollars apiece), and collected all the necessary gaskets and screws I needed to re-assemble the engine. The heater boxes and the tin went to Kombi Haus, where they were cleaned and stripped of their paint. When I got them back, I gave them three coats of paint and let them hang on the fence for a few days so the paint could completely cure.

My first thought was to replace the generator with either an alternator or a rebuilt generator, but I found that there were no rebuilds that matched the amperage of the original bus generator, and that I'd have to substitute one made for a bug. Instead, I decided to keep the original generator but disassemble it and replace the bearings, which are really the only things on a generator that wear out. To do this operation, I needed a puller. Justin had one that lacked only a bolt to be functional, so I borrowed it, bought a new bolt, used the puller, and returned it to him along with the bolt. I also installed new generator brushes, an act which would prove to have lasting consequences, as I later learned.

The rest of the assembly and reinstallation went without a hitch, thanks in large part to a floor jack I borrowed from a neighbor down the street. The only complication I had was that I had had to reshape some of the tin in front of the crankshaft pulley to allow it to clear the new oil filter hose fittings, and the reshaped tin was scraping against the pulley. So I had to pull the pulley off and delicately bang on the tin with a ball-peen hammer and a drift until I could achieve some clearance ... sort of molding the sheet metal in place.

With the new engine installed in my bus, I drove the thing around town for a hundred miles, then changed the oil and oil filter to remove whatever metal particles had been self-machined off the engine during the initial breaking-in period. I also decided to install a new SVDA distributor with the electronic ignition, since I wanted to see how that system performed before I made the trip to a VW gathering in Maupin, Oregon.

I wanted to keep the shake-down trip within two hundred miles of home, and it turned out that a camping trip had been planned for that very weekend up at the Hallsted Campground, near Quincy, California, less than a hundred fifty miles from Sacramento. Some freeway driving, some climbing up into the hills ... it seemed perfect, so off I went.

The route took me up from Sacramento by way of Route 99 and then Route 70, up through Marysville. I had taken this road often in the nineties on trips to Quincy, but there's one section of it that startled me. Route 70 used to be two-lane road and, before it got to Marysville, it passed through the tiny town of East Nicholaus, where there was a four-way stop. There was an ice-cream stand and a roadside fruit stand there, which did a good business since you had to stop there anyway. Now the road was a four-lane highway that bypassed the town entirely. This re-routing happens all the time, of course; there must be a dozen such bypasses on Route 99 between Sacramento and Bakersfield, and they're easy to spot. If I had had a GPS with me, it would have revealed the tell-tale signs of such a re-route: a slight bend in what was otherwise a remorselessly straight line; the older road would still be there as a ghostly presence, usually connected to the new route with an on-ramp and off-ramp. But this one had been done in such a way that you could see no trace of the where the old road ended and the new one began, and there was no direct link to the original road. In only a few short years, the addition had weathered to the point where it was indistinguishable from the old road. The new road provided an access ramp to the road that made up the other segment of that four-way intersection, but that ramp was some distance west of the East Nicholaus itself. If I had not traveled this road before, I would never have known the town was there except for that turnoff west of town. I was seeing "Roadside America" die before my eyes, in the quest for speed and safety.

The trip was thankfully uneventful, as the bus purred up the hills without complaint. I was deliberately not pushing it to its limit while it was so new, so I ended up shifting into third when I might have been tempted to leave it to struggle in fourth gear, but since one couldn't really travel in comfort over forty miles an hour along those mountain roads, it wasn't much of a sacrifice. I found the campsite after only one wrong turn-off, found the other campers, and set up camp.

The only adventure on that particular trip wasn't mine, but Peter's. And that story is told later on in this book as "The Curious Incident of the Bus in the Night-time." Peter's predicament stemmed from a misdiagnosis he'd made, based on some trouble he'd had in the past. It's human nature to assume that when something goes wrong, it's probably the same thing that went wrong before. That same flaw of logic would appear later in my own story, as you will see.

I did have a problem of my own on the way back; the generator light came on. I pulled off the road and Chris Canterbury, who was following me in his own bus, pulled off, too. We both agreed that the light, which signals trouble in the electrical system, had to be due to a faulty voltage regulator that wasn't allowing the battery to charge (the generator tested out OK). I figured that the battery was strong enough to get me home without recharging, so I pressed on.

The next morning, I bought a new voltage regulator, put it in, and found that the problem didn't go away. So I poked around a bit more and found that if I pushed down on the top generator brush, the red light went out and stayed out for a while. I theorized that the brush, being a new one, was having trouble seating on the armature, perhaps because the spring was weak. I replaced that brush with the old one, but that didn't solve the problem so I re-installed the new one. The light went out.

It came on again a few weeks later, when I was on Interstate 84, traveling the south bank of the Columbia River in Oregon. What was I doing at I-84? Well, it's like this. I'd been reading in William Least Heat Moon's *Blue Highways* about a replica of Stonehenge overlooking the Columbia River near the Dalles, and it so happened that I was attending a VW get-together in

Maupin, Oregon, only an hour or two south of there. How could I travel all this way and miss a full-scale model of Stonehenge made of concrete and structural steel? For a lover of off-beat history such as myself, there was really no question. So north I went, and then east about fifteen miles along the Columbia River to where I could cross over to Maryhill, Washington. I found the monument (which is hard to miss, actually, since you can see it as soon as you cross over the bridge) and admired it. There are placards on the columns telling of the soldiers from the area who died in World War I. There were, I think, twenty of them. Most were in their twenties, a couple in their teens, the youngest one a few months shy of his eighteenth birthday.

George at Washington's Stonehenge

That quest completed, I turned east to visit Scott and Jeanne McCartney, two friends of mine from Sacramento who had re-settled in Salem. Scott understands buses. He used to own an extremely rare "barn-door" bus, a pre-1955 version never imported in great numbers. 1955 was the first year Volkswagen imported cars and buses into the U.S. through its own dealership network instead of a variety of importers, so earlier models are now collector's items. (In case you were wondering, the sobriquet came from the bus's huge exterior rear hatch, designed to give access to an area that held not only the engine and battery but the spare tire as well.) By the time he got that bus it had suffered so much damage that he ended up junking it. His second bus caught fire and burned to the ground. He now has a non-running Beetle in his driveway. (When he lived in

Sacramento, he had a non-running VW Squareback in his driveway. I sense a pattern here.)

I entered Scott's address in my new GPS and it told me to get back on I-84 and head west, into a vicious headwind that kept my speed to about fifty but made all the sailboard enthusiasts on the river very happy, I'm sure. Except for the jump start at the rest area, the trip was uneventful except for the red light staying on pretty much all the time.

I arrived at Scott's. but there was nobody home. I checked my cell phone to find a message from Scott that they'd be home a little late, so I read a book and waited. By and by they arrived, we had dinner, and I checked my email and researched repair facilities in Salem.

The next morning, I took out the brush I'd been poking and found that it was half gone. Either I got a bad brush or I somehow turned the generator into a brush-machining lathe when I overhauled it. I went indoors, unfolded the laptop, and looked up a web site called AIRS, which stands for Aircooled Interstate Rescue Service. It lists people all over the United States who volunteer to help drivers of air-cooled Volkswagens who find themselves in need of mechanical help when traveling. A call to the first person listed on the AIRS list was answered by somebody named Brian. It was the first distress call he'd ever gotten. He told me about a VW parts place on the east side of town, and when I called it, I found that the brushes were in stock. Scott drove me out there in his Scion and I spent $7.00 on a pair of brushes. We went back, put the brush in (a vexatious job), and the red light went out and stayed out.

Back on the road. I took SR 22 over the Cascade Range, topping out at around 4800' if I remember right. After Detroit and the spectacular man-made lake there, the road joins US 20 as it meanders down the eastern slope of the Cascades down into Bend, which I arrived at by four o'clock. I made a trip to the library to check my email and recharge my computer, and then had dinner at a Burger King, after which I did some shopping and filled up on gas at the huge Fred Meyer on Business 97.

I had hoped to reach Crescent or at least La Pine by sunset, but that wasn't a realistic goal anymore. A quick reference to the

131

AAA Campbook revealed a campsite supposedly about thirty miles south of Bend called Big Canyon, and off I went in search of it. The directions in the book sucked. It told me to look for a "FR 42" but there seems to be no such road. I ended up at another campground, but they wanted $17 to stay the night, and my stubbornness and stinginess triumphed. I headed back, blundered down a few more roads, and ended up on a side road about where the turnoff should have been. I flagged down some locals, and it turned out that I was on the right road after all. They described a left turn to make, followed by a right turn just past the firehouse, followed by another left turn a few more miles down the road, and I took it all down. None of these directions seemed even remotely like the ones described in the book, and I wondered if they'd sent me on a wild goose chase.

It turns out their directions were right on. I got to the campground right after sunset, giving me one chance to go around the loop, pick out the best vacant spot, get back to the entrance, deposit the site fee into the strong-box there, and get back to the bus before it got too dark to see. As I backed into the slot, I failed to notice a stump sticking out of the ground and rammed it with my bumper, crumpling its right side right into the sheet metal of the quarter panel that Jim Bass had so lovingly restored just last summer. Oh, well, the bumper was bent anyway, and he could repair that when they paint the bus. And I saved $7.00 on the campsite, right?

My next stop was Crater Lake, which I'd wanted to see ever since I moved west. Crater Lake is a great big hole in the ground filled with the bluest water I've ever seen ... a stunning cobalt blue. It is very high up. The altimeter read 7,500 feet as I rounded the crest of the West Rim Road (the East Rim Road was still closed to traffic because of snow, on this twenty-fifth day of June, 2009). There was still a lot of snow piled up at various parts of the Rim Village, notably blocking sidewalks so people had to walk over them. I'm sure that that's where the snow piles were originally, and I suspect they left these walks uncleared so people could later say "I mean, damn, they still had snow on those walks! I had to walk over a mound of snow four feet high just to get on the other side of the sidewalk!" and be greeted by disbelieving or envious stares.

I heard one small child wail "Mom, I'm *tired* of walking!"

There are plenty of overlooks and explanatory placards to tell you about what you're seeing, but it's obvious that the written word is out of its league here. The placards detail how many years old the lake is, how many gallons of water it contains, and so on. You may as well try to "explain" Beethoven's Fifth Symphony with such phrases as: "The breath passing through the wind instruments could fill 1500 balloons; the distance traveled by all the bows of all the stringed instruments, if put end on end, would reach from San Francisco to Sacramento; there are over 27,000 individual notes played by the brass section." I'm making these figures up, of course, but only to make the point that statistics, however charming and amusing they may be, will get you no closer to getting to the reality of Crater Lake than they do for the magnificence of Beethoven's Fifth.

When the placards started repeating themselves as I traveled from one viewpoint to the next, I felt that I'd seen enough of them. I, too, was *tired* of walking. There was an audio-visual presentation at an observation point directly below the Rim Village bookstore; it showed, in time-lapse animation, how Mount Mazama was created and how it self-destructed and left the crater as it is. This observation point's gallery is almost directly above the shoreline, and affords what is probably the best view of Wizard's Island, a cinder cone growing out of the lake bed. There's the usual Indian legend about its origins, no doubt horribly garbled by time and anthropological misunderstanding, so I won't repeat it, but will remark only that it sounds like a lot of other things that have been passed off as Indian legends over the years. Forgive my skepticism.

The bus took it all in stride, and also mostly in third gear. It's a good thing the speed limit along the rim road was only thirty-five, or I would have been obliged to pull over every time a car came up from behind. (I pulled over a few times just the same.) The way down was the same thing: the speed limit was fifty, and the bus seemed perfectly content to do that speed. It

133

came to me that while people speak of driving the car, or driving the road, it's almost always better when you let the car and the road drive you.

With a week's worth of dirty laundry, I stopped in Klamath Falls and found the most spotless laundromat I've ever been in. The machines looked like laundromat machines I've used in the past, except that they took a buck and a half in quarters now, and had little digital screens on them. The driers were still a quarter, but only for about eight minutes now, I found.

I didn't get out of Klamath Falls until after six, and drove around aimlessly looking for a gas station (I don't think I've ever seen a town that hides its gas stations as well as Klamath Falls). The laundromat attendant had told me about a Fred Meyer superstore with a gas station, but her directions didn't make any sense once I got on the road. But not to worry; she'd also told me about a truck stop south of town which was more accessible and only a few cents more expensive, so I gave up the quest for the Fred Meyer and headed south. I found the truck stop. It was closed, out of business, boarded up, kaput. With my gas gauge reading about one-eighth full, I pressed onward, and a few miles north of the California border there was a gas station selling gas for three bucks a gallon. I didn't have much choice, since it was about seventy miles to Weed and I didn't know what was in between. As it turned out, there was another gas station in Dorris, California, a few miles down the road, but the gas was much more expensive ... about $3.30 a gallon, so I did right by filling up.

All these detours made it impossible for me to make it to Whiskeytown, outside Redding, where I planned to camp. So I looked at the AAA CampBook and found a state campground outside Dunsmuir. Twelve bucks a night, coin-op showers, just off the road. It sounded perfect.

The sun had set behind the coast range by the time I passed through Shasta City and Dunsmuir, and I was again racing the twilight. I arrived at Castle Crag State Park to find that the fee was now twenty dollars a night, but at this point it was too dark, and I was too tired, to look for another campground. I filled out

134

the payment envelope in the light of the pay kiosk, stuffed a twenty into it, and went back to the camper in the dark.

Twenty dollars was too much for this campground, I thought. It's pretty enough, and there are flush toilets, but my campsite was only about a hundred yards from Interstate Five, and there was traffic noise all night, much of it loud roars from trucks pulling up the grade into Dunsmuir. I have stayed at rest stops off the freeway that were quieter. Before leaving Castle Crags State Park the next morning, I took a tour of the upper loop of campsites and these proved to be much quieter than the one I had used. The traffic noise was still there, but much more indistinct and muted. I set my the destination on my GPS as Lakeport, where I planned to attend the Lakeport Camp and Shine, a small VW show on the shores of Clear Lake.

On the way down, I had fun with the GPS unit, although if it were a person, it probably would have shot me. Here's why: as I was driving down Interstate 5 in hundred-degree weather, I was overcome by the urge for a chocolate milk shake, the kind you used to be able to get from any number of small ice-cream shops or drive-ins. So I made detours in Orland, Willows, and Maxwell in search of such a place. This involved leaving the highway and driving down the main street of each town, which was usually old Highway 99W. Many years ago, traveling this same road, I had a similar craving for a chocolate shake, and this maneuver had paid off almost immediately, but this time I couldn't find a trace of such an emporium anywhere through my detours. It had almost gotten to the point where I wondered if I had dreamed the earlier incident.

Of course, every time I left the GPS's prescribed route, it would "recalculate" the route based on the last location. It would then tell me to turn left, but I would instead go straight. "Recalculating," it would say. "Go point two miles, then turn left." I would ignore it. "Recalculating. Go point two miles, then turn left." I could swear I detected a note of exasperation as it went through the process again and again. But how do you explain to a little box full of electronics that on a hot summer's day in California's Central Valley, the desire for a cold chocolate milkshake trumps the need to get to Lakeport by the most direct

135

route? Eventually, I would just turn it off and reactivate it once I'd rejoined the traffic on the interstate.

But once I actually paid attention to its directions and followed them, the unit functioned flawlessly and efficiently. My only complaint was the relentlessly cheery voice, which reminded me of the voice of a day-care supervisor. ("Do you know what we're going to do today? We're going to turn right! In one hundred yards, we'll turn left! Won't that be fun?") After fiddling with the optional settings, I replaced it with the prim, no-nonsense voice of a British woman whom I named "Sarah." With this modification, I found that I could get used to this device, particularly in areas where I was a stranger and didn't know the roads.

I got to Lakeport at around seven and checked into the campground by the lake, in the area pre-reserved for the VW people. Chris Canterbury and his family were already there, so I parked next to them. The Kombi Haus people came in a little while later and set up nearby, and Damon and Justin got a chuckle inspecting my bumper remodel. I also met a fellow whom I'll name Mr. Spring, who was handing out fliers as he circulated around the campground. These turned out to be a three-page advertisement for some of the services and products he was offering. The first page, mostly hand-lettered, was a claim that most of the 009 and 094 distributors in VWs were faulty, in that most of them were outfitted with only a single flywheel control spring instead of the two springs for which mountings had clearly been provided by the manufacturer. The lack of this crucial second spring, according to Mr. Spring, would result in premature engine damage. Fortunately, he would equip your distributor with the missing spring for a nominal charge.

Was this true? I went back to my bus and disassembled my spare 009 distributor and, sure enough, there was only one spring although there were clearly two places to mount the spring. Since I found it difficult to believe that thousands of defective distributors had been shipped out without previous complaint, I asked around and found out that the "missing spring" was never intended to be in the distributor. It was true that a second spring might be beneficial to certain applications where one needed to limit the advance, such as in high-performance applications, so mountings had been provided for them. But the second spring was unnecessary for stock ignition configurations.

Later, as I was watching Mr. Spring as he mounted the "missing spring" into somebody's distributor, Justin Campbell came up to me and whispered, "Don't let him sell you a second spring." I would find, after I got back to civilization and researched the subject, that Mr. Spring had been selling these springs for years despite warnings from distributor rebuilders and suppliers that it was so much snake oil. To be fair, the research also turned up a few testimonials from owners of the modified distributors, who said that the modification didn't seem to do any harm and might have even improved the performance of the engine, but the evidence was strictly anecdotal.

I turned in at a little after midnight, and woke up at six-thirty to some techno-reggae-rap music emanating from a few campsites away. Unable to get back to sleep, I made some coffee, toasted some croissants, and tidied up the bus for the show. By and by, we campers trickled over to the city park where the show itself was to be held. It was on the shore of the lake and sported not only picnic tables but wi-fi, allowing me to check my email in the shade of the trees.

The show was over in mid-afternoon, after which we all went back to the campground. The afternoon was crushingly hot, without a wisp of a breeze. I had hoped to do some swimming in the lake, but there seemed to be nothing but scum from the shoreline to about fifty feet out, which was not the most appealing thing to swim in. So I took a cold shower instead and slipped into my swim trunks, which constituted my entire attire from then until bed time.

How hot was it? The little magnetic thermometer in the bus read a hundred five degrees. When Rebecca Canterbury professed astonishment, I got out the thermometer (something Jack had bought years ago) and showed it to her.

"Look, Chris!" she exclaimed to her husband. "It's a little thermometer with a magnet on it!"

"You can buy those things at auto parts stores, I think," Chris replied.

"But this one is so *vintage!*" she said.

And she had a point. There are those bus owners who not only strive to restore their buses to their original showroom state but seek out accessories ... picnic baskets, tableware, Thermos bottles, luggage carriers, suitcases... that are appropriate to that bus's time and place. If these things somehow had the VW emblem on them, so much the better. I met one fellow at Maupin who showed us his version of a portable tape player, designed to fit his early seventies bus. It consisted of a cassette deck of the period mounted in an enclosure with two speakers of the same period, and powered with lantern batteries ... a far cry from an iPod, but certainly matching the rest of his stuff. And, of course, the tapes all had sixties and seventies music on them.

I came home with two prizes for the show. One was "First Place" for my class, which was Stock Bay Window. I think there were only two stock Bays, and the other one, which was Chris Canterbury's, was very much a work in progress. The other was "Second Place" for distance traveled. The first place entrant came from a hundred seventy-nine miles away. I came in second with one thousand, four hundred and forty-eight miles. (The judges said that even though I had come from Sacramento, which is only about a hundred thirty miles away, the fact that I had taken the long way around should have earned me at least an honorable mention.)

A week after I got home, the generator light went out for good. I wondered if it had gone out some time ago and I just hadn't noticed it before. This was disquieting, because if the light had gone out, the generator might have been playing its old tricks again without me noticing. I ran a few of the diagnostic procedures described in the Idiot Book and eliminated the voltage regulator as the source of the trouble. So it had to be either the generator or the bulb itself. I unscrewed the speedometer cable and removed the instrument cluster from the dashboard (thinking that I was getting pretty good at this by now), yanked out the bulb, and tested it. Yup, it was bad. So the bulb got replaced with a new one. A few months earlier, I had read about a replacement bulb that was available for the dash lights that was a wee bit brighter than the originals, which always shed a maddeningly dim glow. (The old buses were notorious for this. Even with both of the dashboard bulbs active, one could barely see the display in anything but total darkness, and if one of them burned out, you lost illumination on that entire side of the instrument cluster.) I'd bought four of the new bulbs, and took the opportunity to replace the dash light bulbs along with the generator warning light and the high-beam indicator, since they all use the same bulb. After hooking up the battery again and starting the car, I found the generator light working in the ignition switch's test position and continuing to glow a bit once the engine turned over, but it went out when I revved the engine and stayed out as the car returned to idle, indicating that the charging system was working.

Another thing I replaced was the rear bumper. I'd had it with the one that crumpled so easily at the campsite in Oregon, so I took it off and substituted one made of a wooden fence post, just like the "bomper" on the Blunder Bus and the Thunder Bus. I would replace that bumper a few months later with one that had a mounting for a trailer hitch ball welded to it, for use in towing a small trailer I had.

A few months later, I took my bus to a meeting. When I started the bus for the ride home, the generator light went on and stayed on. Now it had been coming on before when I started the bus, and I asked Justin about it. It was normal, he said, as the voltage regulator sometimes needed a spike of voltage to kick in, but was nothing to worry about as long as it went out when the engine was revved. I watched its behavior after that; it would go out and stay out after I revved the engine. But not this time.

The following morning, I decided to trouble-shoot the problem. I first looked at the upper generator brush, the one I had replaced last June. Giving the brush a little "goosing" – the little push I put on it when it was acting up before – had no effect, so I took it out to inspect it visually. It looked fine, so I re-installed it (a vexatious job requiring much swearing at the brush and at the designer and at the neighbor's dog, who was barking incessantly at the squirrels in his back yard).

The problem was the screws that hold the brushes in place. This was because the holes the screws went into are recessed about a half an inch inside the generator, mostly out of sight but with lots of empty space beneath it where a screw could be dropped. If that happened, you'd never get it out without dismantling the generator completely. So it is imperative that the screw not part company with the screwdriver until it is threaded into the hole. I accomplished this by taping the screw to the screwdriver with electrical tape; as the screw was seated, I could then pull the screwdriver away from the screw and strip the tape from either the screw or the screwdriver. But even with the tape, the screw was free to wobble on the end of the screwdriver, making it difficult to thread into the hole. I vowed that the next time those screws came out, they would be replaced by Allen-head cap screws, which do a better job of staying put on the wrench that's used to tighten them.

To make matters worse, you cannot see the screw and its hole without a mirror, which must be angled in such a way as to show what's going on with the screw. If you try this, you immediately find that the mirror shows you a reverse image: left and right preserve their proper orientation, but when you try move the screwdriver forward, it instead goes backward. My dentist may be used to maneuvering tools this way, but I'm not. So a job that should take only thirty seconds took ten exasperating minutes.

Getting out my volt-ohmmeter, I did the diagnostic stuff to determine whether it was the voltage regulator or the generator that was bad. The diagnostic routine said it was the generator. I wasn't so sure. Somehow I couldn't believe that the generator, so recently overhauled, could be at fault. I suspected the voltage regulator, even though it was new. Well, I had the regulator I took out of the bus last spring, so I switched it out with the new one. I had lost the screw that went into the D-minus (or generator ground) terminal, and didn't have another one, so I tapped it out to fit a 10-24 threaded screw that I did have. (This is the sort of thing that drives restorers crazy, because they expect to find a metric screw there, and if some future owner in turn lost the screw, the last replacement he would expect would be one with American threads. But I thought that if the voltage regulator was indeed bad, I'd be replacing it with a new one and retiring the original back to the spares box.)

It's not easy to replace the voltage regulator in a '71 bus. The earlier buses, and the VW beetles, had their regulators perched right on top of the generator, but the early bay-window buses tucked them into the deepest part of the right side of the engine compartment, where the air-cleaner pedestal and the fan housing blocked easy access. As I struggled with the screws and terminals on it, I envisioned evil-minded designers conspiring to complicate what should have been a simple task:

Designer Number 1: "See what I have done here, Horst? I have put the regulator where it is very difficult to use a screwdriver to attach it to the frame. Isn't this marvelous?"

Designer Number 2: "That is indeed an excellent placement, Dieter! I especially like the way you have located it in the darkest part of the compartment, so one must use a flashlight to see what he is doing."

Designer Number 1: "But that is the beauty of it! There is no place to put a flashlight! There is not even enough space to put one's hand in to connect the terminals, unless one has the hands of a six-year-old! To put another hand there to hold a flashlight is quite impossible!"

Designer Number 2: "*Ausgezeichnet!* You are a genius! But may I suggest that if we lower the air-cleaner pedestal by two centimeters, it will obscure the view of the lower screw completely, as well as further obstruct access."

Designer Number 1: "What a wonderful suggestion, Horst! That will certainly earn you an extra knackwurst next payday!"

At last the voltage regulator went in and I hooked everything up, but when I started the car, the red light leered malevolently at me again and refused to go out. I ran the diagnostics again, and got the same result as before. Now I could at least believe that what the instruments were telling me was a good regulator was indeed a good regulator. That left the generator.

I was in denial about the generator primarily because replacing it involved taking the engine out again. I had a sudden thought: what if I "goosed" the lower generator brush, the one I hadn't replaced?

I goosed it.

The light went out.

So I took the lower generator brush out of the car and installed the partner of the upper brush I replaced last June (they're sold in pairs, and this is why). The old lower brush was worn down quite a bit, but not to the extent that the upper one had been. I took the bus over to our local drive-in burger shack to see if the light would go off and stay off. It did, so I considered the problem fixed, at least for now, and bought another set of brushes as spares.

I had, of course, fallen into a classic conceptual trap. My diagnosis had been based on my previous experience with the failure mode of a generator brush, which was gradual; I could not believe that the same malady had befallen my bus again, but that the failure mode was different. So, ruling out what was obviously the problem, I had instead substituted a diagnosis that conformed to my expectations rather than the evidence. This cost me extra work, and will probably cost me more extra work when that voltage regulator again fails and I'll have to replace it with the newer one. I'm almost hoping that the engine will have to come out before then, making that replacement a whole lot easier, but this is really not the sort of wish that I actually want to come true, at least for several thousand more miles.

This is not to say that the entire week was spent trouble-shooting. I was also crafting another storage cabinet for my bus, to be fitted over the recess where the spare tire was originally stored. The raw material came from another cabinet that Bob Frith had given me, which we pulled out of one of his parts buses. The material was delaminating, and its bottom edge showed some dry rot, but there was enough decent material left to make the cabinet I had in mind. It would even use the standard cabinet door that came with it. It took a bit of relaminating, cutting and fitting, but I eventually had a cabinet that, at first glance, would pass for something that could have could have come from the Westfalia factory as standard equipment. When I showed it to Peter the next time I saw him, he at first took it for one I'd scored from some right-hand-drive Westfalia. When I told him the truth, he exclaimed, "You *hacked* it?" I had a proud moment there. Jack MacNeil would have approved.

Meanderings

Whenever I embark on a trip, thoughts come to my mind of all the long-distance driving I've done in VWs. There is one common thread to them all: the imperative of Getting There.

"Getting There" differs from simply "getting there." The latter is the aim of the journey, of course. That's why we've set out in the first place. But when one feels the need to travel just a little farther, the urgency to reach a goal by a certain time, to put just a few more miles between you and your starting point, then "getting there" has become Getting There.

You rationalize it, just as you rationalize other failings of character. You say that whatever extra distance you make tonight is distance that you won't have to drive tomorrow. Tomorrow will be more leisurely, slower-paced, you promise yourself (a promise you know you will break even as you're making it). Or you say that it would be nice to get home a few hours earlier than you otherwise would have. Isn't that an inviting thought? This line of reasoning is especially persuasive after dark, when you are no longer enjoying the view of the scenery sliding past. One mile of freeway at night looks pretty much like any other mile, and twenty miles may as well be thirty miles, or forty miles, or more.

It's even more pernicious when you have some good music with you. At night, there's nothing like cranking up Mike Oldfield's "Ommadawn" or Beethoven's Ninth Symphony and letting the music choreograph the miles, particularly when you're driving through lonely stretches of the high desert with only your headlights and the moon for illumination. These are the conditions that invite driving long beyond the point where you should have pulled over. My cousin Ray Guido fell asleep at the wheel in such a situation, and died. I think about that sometimes when I've been driving too long, too far. It is true that there is beauty in being immersed in music as you weave your way through the darkness, but there is always the potential of a horrible price to be paid for that beauty.

Getting There, if left unrecognized and untreated, can spoil the fun in other ways. In your headlong rush to get somewhere, you pass up all the little side trips that can make a journey rewarding. The only cure is to leave the freeway and drive down some two-lane road that the locals know about. That's where you'll find the good diners, the little stores that somehow hang on in the era of the Big Box, or the roadside parks.

One good antidote for Getting There is a vehicle that won't let you get away with much. That's why a VW Bus makes such a good road boat (I suspect that many of the RVs you see on the road fall into that category as well.) You won't speed because you can't. Since you're in the slow lane anyway, and doomed to remain there for the foreseeable future, you don't mind taking longer looks out the window and slowing down a little more for a particularly enchanting view. Of course, driving at night cancels out that advantage, so one has to be more alert to the danger. And indeed, I found that the urge to Get There was much stronger once the sun went down. It helps to have a co-driver; with two people sharing the driving, neither one of you will get dangerously close to fatigue, and you'll usually be talking anyway to pass the time.

On my many solo drives around the nation, I haven't always been able to overcome the primal need to Get There. Like a recovering alcoholic, you can't say you've really been cured. But on every trip, I try to take the time to investigate some little side road or roadside attraction, like a museum or an historical landmark. It may not get me there faster, but it makes getting there more worthwhile to me.

Over the past few years, I've put about thirty thousand miles on George. Most of that mileage consisted of numerous campouts with my local VW cronies. We'd show up at a campground with anywhere from three to fifteen buses and find an area of our own away from the other campers, who had motor homes or fifth-wheel campers – large, ponderous contraptions usually given names of Indian tribes or birds (and why is such a huge vehicle named after a small delicate bird like the Sandpiper?). We'd set up a large rain fly over one of the firepits, which would give us about three hundred square feet of warm, dry space even when the weather wasn't cooperating. I brought the first of these shelters, but other campers in our group eventually came up with their own.

I took a few longer trips, too. One began badly, but ended well.

There was a time when I was towing a trailer to an event in Arizona. I had replaced the fence-post bumper with one equipped with a tow hitch installed to a plate welded onto the bumper itself. It didn't look very strong, so I reinforced the bumper with a piece of square pipe. I towed the empty trailer with this setup, and everything seemed to go smoothly. Since it was a small trailer, and I was only going to put about five hundred pounds of stuff into it, I figured that everything would work out. What I hadn't counted on was that when a trailer goes over a speed bump, it creates momentary strains on the tongue that far exceed the normal load.

My travel plans lasted exactly one hundred and fourteen miles. I left Sacramento at around ten o'clock in the morning, and stopped for lunch in Merced. When I went back to my bus, I found to my horror that the trailer's tongue had bent the bumper downwards. The right bumper mount had actually bent ninety degrees downward, and the left one was severely tweaked. It was obvious that I was not going to get to Arizona and back with this arrangement. I towed the trailer very, very carefully to the house of a friend who lived nearby, unhooked it, and proceeded to Arizona. A week later, I retrieved the trailer and towed it home with the Sienna, which had a trailer hitch.

My friends told me that the stock bumper brackets were too weak to support the load of a trailer hitch, but that they could be modified by "boxing" them, which consists of welding an additional plate across the bottom of the U-shaped bracket to prevent the sides from distorting. I had this done, but didn't get a chance to test the modification until the following fall, when I again towed the laden trailer to a woodworking demonstration. This time, the brackets did fine, but the bumper itself bent at the point where the reinforcing square pipe ended. I replaced that pipe with a longer piece that spread the tow load over the entire bumper, from bracket to bracket. Later one, I would add two more attachment points directly over the bumper brackets themselves, to which I could attach the single-wheel trailer I'd bought.

I also repeated my trip up to Maupin for the 2010 RendezVW, which was pretty much like the last one except that Joe Ehrlich had also made the trip this year. We camped together, and he found himself being the unofficial spokesman for my bus, answering all sorts of questions about the Dormobile top when I wasn't around. Joe also owned one of the sweetest dogs I've ever met, a female pit bull mix named Maggie. Maggie was always a hit with children, who would drag her around, ride her, and smother her with attention, causing Joe to sometimes wonder if he wasn't better known as Maggie's owner than in his own right. I told him that I felt the same about my bus as he did about Maggie, since it invariably attracts more attention than I do,

After that, there were no more long trips that year... just a visit to a Sierra campsite on BLM land at nine thousand feet; the usual fall get-together at Finnon Lake, where I'd first met the people I'd be camping with for the next eight years; and a couple of other campouts that fall. I also took my sister on an overnight campout in Sonoma County, not far from where my brother lived; she had been visiting him for a week before returning to her own home in Texas, and wanted to have at least one camping experience with me to complement the trip we had taken almost forty years ago in my Pink Bus to Shenandoah National Park. This time she had her own tent, and no bears were around, but some creature (most likely a dog owned by some other campers) woke her in the night, and I agreed that it could have been a coyote, or even a bear, if that's what she wanted to believe.

I also attended a pre-Thanksgiving dinner held at the Bothe-Napa State Park, where we had cooked and eaten a turkey dinner with all the trimmings at the campground, huddled under a large sunshade while a storm dumped a few inches of rain, and toasted friends absent and present, including Joe Ehrlich (who

147

was at that moment in China, teaching schoolchildren how to speak English with an American accent). Despite the weather, we stayed pretty dry and reasonably sober, although we had to burn about a quarter cord of wood over the course of that weekend. There's a group of VW campers up in the Pacific Northwest called the "Wet Westies," who pride themselves in camping in rainy conditions. Well, they had no reason to feel more smug than we did that weekend.

Over the years, I've been back to the RendezVW in Oregon and Buses by the Bridge in Arizona, although I missed two of those events due to an illness of mine or a death in the family. And I've been on many, many other trips with the friends I'd met over the years. Of those trips, there are a few that stand out.

Fort Bragg Blues

One year, I descended the hill coming into Fort Bragg, California from Willits on Route 20. I was still wondering if this trip was worth it ... a long, hot drive from Sacramento to camp in a place I'd never been to, on the property of some people I hadn't met. All that concern evaporated when my brakes started to fail.

Route 20 is not one of those roads you want to be on with wonky brakes. The speed limit is 55, which is laughable when there is a hairpin turn every few hundred yards that requires you to slow down to thirty, or twenty, or even slower. Add to that a healthy grade – you're dropping about a half a mile of elevation in about five miles of road – and you've got a situation where you're going to be using your brakes a lot, and using them hard ... if you had them.

If you didn't, or at least not enough of them, then it's a bit more challenging. You end up downshifting a lot, trying to be as easy on the brakes as you can. And you pray that the traffic behind you won't ride your bumper. You look for turnouts even where there are no turnouts, so you can pull off the road and let the others pass you. Naturally, you find that every time you're forced to use a marginal strip of gravel that leaves you skidding to a stop, and you let the traffic pass, you will find a perfectly good turnout around the next corner, wide and paved and completely invisible until you're almost past it. Sometimes the turnouts are well marked. And sometimes they're not.

And that's the way I continued down the hill. By the time I arrived at the bottom, what was left of my front brake pads had machined themselves into oblivion. That's when I started hearing the grinding noise that indicates that the pads are gone and that the metal that the pads used to be on is now in contact with the rotor. I coasted into town at a painfully slow speed, using the parking brake to ooze to a stop whenever I needed to.

I checked my cell phone. Crappy Sprint. There was no coverage in Fort Bragg. My only hope was to find an internet connection somewhere. I saw a sign that said that a library was three blocks off the main drag. I drove there. It was closed, due to budget cuts.

As I carried my computer back to the car, I passed a cafe. It had wi-fi. I grabbed a table and opened up the computer. As I feared, there was no shop specializing in VW parts, but some friendly locals in a Vanagon directed me to a brake shop that had a good reputation. I went there to find the proprietor locking it up for the weekend. He told me he didn't have the parts, but I could probably get them from the auto parts store around the corner, which was open late. So I went there and ordered a new set of disc brake pads, which they promised would be there the next morning. I remembered that Peter, who had plans to be at that same campout, had told me that he wouldn't be driving up the coast until Saturday morning, so I made arrangements to have him pick up the parts and bring them to the campsite.

The campsite was about twelve miles away, and I managed to get there without using the brakes much at all. It was level most of the way, with only a few intimidating turns. Once I got off the main road, it was pretty much out of the question to shift out of first or second gear, so I counted on engine braking to slow me down when necessary.

The campsite was a large open meadow, populated by two horses and a few dozen sheep, and no other campers there at all; it turned out I was the first one there. In a little while, somebody else showed up, a very nice fellow from Arcata named Bob. We were joined by the landowner, who turned out to be associated

149

with the microbrewery in Fort Bragg. He'd seen the vehicles in the field and came down to let us know that Melissa, who had actually organized the campout, had experienced some delays and wouldn't arrive until the following morning.

Nobody's cell phone worked where we were, so Jon, the landowner, let me use his land line to call Peter. I got Peter's voicemail and left a message instructing him to stop by the auto parts store on his way up and pick up my brake pads. Later, he retrieved the message and left word on Jon's voicemail that he'd be glad to. I set up camp and made dinner. Finally, things were going well, and I took it as a sign that my problems would soon be over.

Fat chance. After breakfast, I started taking the front brakes apart. Off went the tire. On the car's left side, I found that the outside brake pad was entirely gone. I'd need new pads, for sure. But it looked like the rotors themselves were in fine shape, which meant that luck smiled on me again ... I'd caught it just in time.

Peter arrived with the pads. They weren't the right ones. In fact, they were about half the area of the originals, and the mounting holes weren't the same. I walked up to Jon's house and called the parts store

"I was afraid of that," the parts guy said. "But since I wasn't 100% sure I'd ordered the right parts for your car, I also ordered another set at the same time. It looks like your '71 bus had '73 calipers installed at some time. Bring the first set back, and I'll swap them for the other set."

So Bob took me into town in his Vanagon, which had an Audi engine in it. That thing could go. We found the parts store, and the swap was made. These pads had the proper surface area, and I was sure they'd fit.

They didn't fit. They were too thick. Or maybe I couldn't compress the pistons far enough back into the calipers to allow the pads to slip in. Since we were at a standstill anyway, I went ahead and split the left-side caliper assembly to find out why that pad wore out so quickly while there was still plenty of material left on the other pads.

It turned out that the caliper has been overheated, and the piston appeared to be seized. There was one way to find out for sure. Like many farmers and ranchers, Jon had a machine shop to keep all the equipment functioning, and among his shop equipment was a press. We took the half-caliper over to his shop, Jon put it in the press, and he pushed the piston back into the caliper. Even though the piston boot looked scorched, the piston moved fairly freely.

That changed the picture quite a bit. If I put everything back together again like it was, with all the old pads reinstalled, that piston would continue to push what was left of the brake pad, now totally bereft of whatever they make pad linings from, into the rotor. Rotors are very expensive things to replace, if they're available at all. But would I have to take that chance in order to be able to drive home?

Maybe not, Jon thought. Maybe we could just block the brake fluid gallery, the passageway in the caliper that supplies brake fluid to that piston. That would immobilize the piston, so that it couldn't push the brake pad into the rotor. We decided to tap some threads into the gallery and fit some set screws in there. That woud do the trick. Of course, it would mean that the left disc brake would be at only half efficiency. It would also, I find out later, ruin the caliper's chances to be rebuilt. But at the moment, it seemed like a small price to pay for saving the rotor.

The set screws were fitted and glued into place with thread-locking compound, and I reassembled the brakes. The next morning, I test drove the car around the meadow and found that while it was a bitch to keep the car going straight when the brakes were applied hard, the car was both drivable and stoppable.

I was invited to stay an extra day, but I wanted to get back home, and it seemed likely that the traffic wouldn't be as bad on Sunday as it would be on Monday, particularly around the version of Hell that is US 101 going from Windsor to San Rafael. (Needless to say, I would not be taking Route 20 back to Sacramento; I was pressing my luck as it was without inflicting that steep winding road on my brake-impaired bus.)

The trip home turned out to be uneventful. I used the freeways as much as I could and therefore didn't have to brake too much. I chose US 101 south to San Rafael, then 37 to I-80.

The only place where I had to use my brakes a lot was in the stretch between Santa Rosa and San Rafael, where the construction delays are continual, even on weekends.

The next day, the old brake calipers came off and I called Kombi Haus. Justin ordered new calipers for me but when I picked them up, I found that they don't match the brake pads I had. It turned out that I had the stock '71 calipers and disk pads all along. The original set that Peter picked up from Acme weren't for a bus at all, but probably for a Karmann Ghia or Porsche. So now I was stuck with a set of brake pads for a '73 or later Transporter, and I needed to get the proper ones to fit the proper calipers.

All of which arrived the next day. This time I really did have what I need, and I installed the calipers and brake pads. The day after that, my friend Tom came over and stomped on the brake pedal while I bled the brakes. At long last, I was back on the road.

A Hard Rain's a-Gonna Fall

Another campout that was out of the ordinary happened in March of 2011. We wanted a memorable campout, and we got one.

Of the eight people who originally planned to attend Ralph's Sugarloaf Ridge campout, four of us refused to believe the weather reports of a storm moving in. A similar storm had been predicted for the previous week, but that storm didn't happen, so we decided to chance it. And so it was that Mike, Jeff, and I arrived at the park on Friday afternoon. Ralph was late, having had some car trouble in Pleasant Hill.

Mike was first to arrive. When I showed up a half an hour later, we went into the park and found that the camping area we originally had in mind, in the upper area of the park, had been blocked. So we parked the buses and walked around checking out the remaining campsites.

None of them were ideal. Some already showed signs of flooding in the rains we'd had that day and the preceding one. Others didn't have enough room between the trees to set up the

Tent of Doom, a large protective rain-fly I often bring to these campouts. Still others had absurdly tall firepits, almost up to our hips, which required far more wood to burn efficiently. At last we decided on a campsite near the new toilet/shower building, which had barely enough space to set up the tent. As I drove the stakes in, I noticed that the ground on the south side of the tent was extremely soft and damp. But reasoned that, as long as the winds didn't come from the south or southeast, we would probably be okay.

We were sitting around the fire on Friday night when Ralph finally showed up. He didn't like our choice of campsite, because the lights were on all night in the shower/toilet building, so he chose another one some distance away.

When the ranger came by to check us in, she mentioned that the low bridge that led into the campground might be flooded if the rains got worse, and advised us to move our cars into another part of the park where there would be no danger of our not being able to get out. But she wasn't very emphatic about it, and told us that if the creek really started to rise, she'd come by again and let us know, so we stayed put. With the big tent up, we were reasonably comfortable, although I kicked myself later that night for not bringing my portable heater, since the temperature dropped precipitously at nightfall and never really warmed up again until Sunday.

It rained all that night, and when I got up, I noticed that the creek hadn't risen enough to flood the bridge. In fact, I walked across it to get to the park's visitor center, where I had a nice talk with Dave Chalk, the docent. Dave was a retired schoolteacher from Michigan who splits his time between that state and California, avoiding California summers and Michigan winters. He, too, told me that the bridge had flooded in the past. Back in the eighties, a fellow driving a Nissan pickup truck had attempted to ford the creek at the bridge and found himself swept downstream, eventually lodging in a ravine where it was unrecoverable by tow vehicles. It was eventually chopped up into small pieces by a band of Eagle scouts and removed, piece by piece, to clear the stream. I wondered if our buses would be able to avoid such a fate. They were considerably heavier, after all, and it was possible that we could make the ford as long as the water wasn't up to the level of our buses' crankcases and heads. I bought another bundle of firewood at the kiosk to supplement the one I'd brought in from outside and walked back to camp. It turned out that Jeff and Mike were walking in the opposite direction and decided to buy another bundle of firewood apiece. We decided to stay for the second night.

As the afternoon progressed, the stream started to rise steadily, and by three o'clock the water level was probably eight inches over the bridge. So we were pretty much trapped until the water level went back down, which the rangers said would be by Saturday evening or Sunday morning, if the rain didn't get worse.

The rain got worse.

It got so bad, in fact, that I fished out the weather-band radio I carried for just such emergencies, and switched it on. The news wasn't good. The barometer was falling, a huge storm was moving in, and more rain was expected, along with winds of about forty knots, gusting to sixty at times. And, of course, these winds would be from the southeast, directly down the canyon where we were camped.

By five o'clock in the afternoon, the stream level hadn't dropped an inch. But at least it hadn't risen further, giving us some hope that it would fall enough by Sunday morning to let us out. To keep out the worst of the wind, we rigged some plastic tarps on the open end of the tent, and that allowed us a modicum of shelter from the elements, although there was still enough swirling wind inside the tent to make for a draft on the fire that was fitful at best. I found that I couldn't stand very long before the smoke got to my eyes. But standing was really the only way we could get heat from that badly designed firepit ... not one of the tallest ones on the campsite, but still not low enough to warm us properly. At about nine in the evening, I gave up, made my excuses, and retired for the night. The rain kept falling.

The storm the weather radio told us about finally hit at around midnight, or a little later. It announced its arrival with winds rising from a moan to a howl and finally a roar. Gusts hit

154

the bus, rocking it back and forth. Sometimes the gusts would arrive with some warning, preceded by an increase in wind noise giving me about five to fifteen seconds to brace myself. At other times, it would come out of nowhere, slamming into the bus. I realized that I could no longer hear the creek, whose overflowing waters had been providing us with a sort of white-noise generator all that day and evening. The wind, it seemed, had become a huge playful cat, and I was the mouse. I could only hope that the wind might become bored with the game, but an hour had passed since the advent of the storm and it had not abated in the slightest.

I simply didn't know what to do. Should I get dressed, so that I would be prepared in case I had to leap out of the car in the middle of the night and batten down hatches, or would I be better off staying inside my sleeping bag and trying to get a little sleep? Should I drop the pop top or leave it be? I feared that the wind would damage the bellows and vinyl. On the other hand, if a gust came up just as I had released the struts but before I lowered the top, the top would be even more vulnerable to damage. In the end, I did nothing, trusting that since it hadn't collapsed yet, the odds were with me that it could survive the storm.

I looked out the window occasionally to check on the tent, just visible in what light from the full moon was penetrating the clouds. Miraculously, it stayed up. A tree to the south was just close enough to provide something of a windbreak, and the line of trees on the other side of the creek provided additional protection. Still, you could hear the wind luffing the fabric and making the ropes thrum.

At about two-thirty, the storm started to ease up, turning into a steady rain. It wasn't quite over yet; the cat had not yet tired of her game. There were periods of calm where I could actually hear the sound of the stream again, and the winds were light. Then the cat would come back and bat us around a little more. It was another hour before she got bored and left us for good. I fell asleep.

In the morning, I got dressed, put some water on the stove for coffee and oatmeal, and then took a walk down to the stream.

It was even higher than it had been the day before, now covering the entire bridge instead of just the middle (for some reason, the bridge had been built with a dip instead of an arch in the middle). Not good. There was ample evidence of the storm's intensity all around the campground, with several trees missing large branches and one tree split in two, not to mention smaller branches strewn everywhere. So I went back to camp, had breakfast, and listened to the weather radio.

The morning's news was marginally better than the previous night's. The worst of the storm was indeed over; the barometer was rising again, and "showers and light rains" were called for, with light winds from the west. The next big storm wasn't due until Monday evening at the earliest. It would still be cold ... hovering in the high forties. But the amount of rainfall was still the big question. The rangers had told us on Saturday that if the rains were light, the creek would eventually go down. We had counted on that, but the rains instead had gotten harder overnight. Now, on Sunday morning, the rain was lighter but more or less constant. It didn't look likely that the stream would ebb faster than the rainwaters could replenish it.

After breakfast, I went back to the bridge to take some pictures of the flood. The person who operated the kiosk was on the other side, and we chatted for a little while, barely making ourselves heard over the roar of the water. She said that the creek was higher than she'd ever seen it in the three years she'd been there. I noticed that somebody had erected a barrier on the other side of the bridge, and asked her if it would be removed once the bridge became passable. The barrier was just visible from our campsite, and its disappearance would be our clue to start preparing to get out. She said not to count on it. Instead, it was better to keep an eye on the bridge ourselves and, when it got low enough for us to ford, to simply move the barrier aside and replace it once we'd gone through.

With nothing better to do, Mike and Jeff and I wandered around the park, looking for place where we could get cell phone coverage. I finally found a place where I could pick up Sprint service, in the higher loop of the campground that had been closed to vehicles. But Mike and Jeff, with their iPhones and

AT&T service, couldn't find a signal. I called my wife to tell her that I might be late getting home – a lot late, in fact, maybe a day or two late. I had enough food in the car for another day, but nothing after that, so I was hoping that we'd be out of the park by Monday evening at the latest. But that all depended on the creek, and on the rain.

The next few hours were spent in a leisurely pack-up, with occasional strolls down to the bridge to check the progress of the flood. By mid-afternoon, the rain had ceased completely and we could see the water level drop by a half an inch an hour. We figured that if the level had dropped to lower than eight inches, we'd attempt to ford the stream. If not, we'd resign ourselves to another night.

Or maybe not. At around four, the lady who mans the kiosk told us that she'd heard that there was another storm on the way, which was expected to arrive that evening. This was news to me, since it didn't jibe with the NOAA weather report I'd heard that morning, but I figured that her information (which came from the ranger station) had to be better than mine, since the rangers had more experience with interpreting the microclimate of the area. By five-thirty, we decided that we'd chance the stream whether or not it continued to fall. So we struck the big tent, which was nearly dry by that time, and finished packing.

In the hang gliding world, there's something known as a "wind dummy." When a group of pilots goes to a flying site, it's usually the most experienced one who launches first, the idea being that he or she is best capable of dealing with any unseen turbulence or other adverse conditions. The others would watch that pilot and, if nothing seemed amiss, they in turn would launch more or less in the order of their skill in the sport. The only exception was the last pilot, who was generally more skilled but who would remain to advise the others if conditions looked like they might change.

We talked about who the "ford dummy" would be. Ralph elected to go first, possibly because he felt comfortable doing it, or because he was the one whose idea this campout was in the first place. I would go next, because I had done this sort of thing in the past with Blunderbus and, if Ralph made it through, he could always tow me out if I stalled. Then came Mike, and then Jeff.

At around six o'clock, we gave the creek a final survey. It hadn't gone down much further, but it hadn't risen, either, and if another storm was really on the way, it looked like our best chance, so we took it.

Ralph's Vanagon forded the stream without difficulty, and there didn't even seem to be any great sideways pressure from the force of the water, so I breathed a little easier. He moved the barrier aside and motioned us over. The trip across the bridge was a piece of cake. None of the remaining three cars had the slightest bit of trouble. When I arrived at the other side, I got out and looked over the bus; the bottom of the tailpipe was wet, possibly from water kicked up by the tires, but the top was dry. We replaced the barrier, shook hands, and went our separate ways. I stopped at my brother's house in Sonoma, where he and his wife fed me dinner and coffee. I arrived home at about ten, took a shower, went to bed, and slept for twelve hours.

And that's pretty much the whole story, at least from my point of view. The next day, the sun was shining and the weather was reasonably warm, so I set up the tent enough to dry it out the rest of the way and unpacked the bus. I'd camped out in storms many times over the years but, with the exception of a folk festival in 1971, when a girlfriend and I rode out the tail end of Hurricane Agnes in a two-man Army pup tent, I think that this was probably the worst one in its duration and wind velocity. I decided that I'll go back to Sugarloaf Ridge sometime, but probably not in the rainy season, and not without paying more attention to the weather forecasts.

A Ferry to Nowhere

And then there was the campout in 2012, on the weekend of the Superbowl. I decided to spend some time with my friends at a campground near Rio Vista, California, a town that is nestled in the labyrinth of waterways that mark the Sacramento River's metamorphosis into the upper San Francisco Bay. It's a good time to go camping, because the campgrounds are largely deserted; all the sportsmen are home watching the Big Game. This was the same campsite I visited in early 2009, when I gave George's original engine its last long trip before being replaced.

The Sandy Beach campground is usually around an hour's drive from my house in Sacramento. You can get there either by heading south on Interstate Five, picking up Highway Twelve, and heading west to Rio Vista. Or you can take the way I go, by way of West Sacramento. This way is actually two minutes shorter, according to my GPS, and much more scenic, since it takes you on a series of back roads and levee roads, through fields and wetlands. It even includes a ride on one of the remaining free ferries operated by the California Department of Transportation. I'd discovered that route last year, when I programmed the campground's address into my GPS and let it guide me through the back roads.

I remembered some of the route from a trip I'd taken to the campground a few years ago. I didn't trust my memory to re-create the path, so I left it once again in the hands of Sarah, the GPS lady. But this time it was Sarah's turn to be mistaken.

All went well until I came to the Ryer Island ferry. It was closed. Not closed for lunch, not closed for the holidays, just closed. There was a chain across the entrance, and no indication of how a detour might be negotiated.

Well, things like this have happened before. I'd usually drive on a little further, and the GPS would eventually select another route that would get me there. No problem. And, as I expected, Sarah started "recalculating" and told me to drive a ways farther and take a left. And so I did, onto a road that had definitely seen better days. I was towing my single-wheel trailer, so I had to pay some attention to the condition of the center of the lane, which usually can be safely ignored.

Maybe I was paying entirely too much attention to the condition of the center lane, because I didn't realize that Sarah was sending me on a long circular route. After twenty minutes, I found myself on a road that looked very familiar. There was even a Caltrans truck parked off the road that looked just like the one I'd passed a half an hour ago. And then there was that driveway that dropped dramatically down from the levee road to a farmhouse and shed ... I'd seen that before, too. Could it be?

It was. In another five miles, I was back at the ferry.

If there was a way I could have programmed Sarah to look for another way to Rio Vista, which didn't involve the ferry, I couldn't remember how to do it. So I used the navigator of last resort, a map of central California that had just enough information to chart a new path.

While I was looking at the map, another car came by and stopped. Inside was a young woman whose GPS had guided her to the same ferry. I explained that the ferry was closed, but that there was another route that looked promising. She made a call on her cell phone, hoping to talk to somebody who could clear up the problem, but there was no answer at the other end.

At this point, I told her that I was going to try the route I'd found, and that she'd be welcome to follow me. And off I went. She followed me for about a mile, but then I lost her in my rear-view mirror. I suspect that she'd decided to trust her GPS the same way I did, and let it steer her on the same roundabout wild-goose chase I'd taken. Well, I couldn't blame her. Given the choice of trusting either the device she'd come to depend on or some creepy old guy in a Volkswagen bus, what could I expect?

The alternate route led me to another free ferry, a smaller cable ferry that put me on a main road southward that linked up with Route Twelve just a mile or so from the great drawbridge across the Sacramento River that links Rio Vista to points east. And a few minutes later, I was at the campground, only an hour later than I'd planned. Well, actually, a little more than an hour, since I'd stopped at a McDonald's and used their wi-fi to post the news of the ferry's closure to the campers who hadn't yet left their homes.

I found out later that the Ryer Island ferry had been closed on and off for the past year. A new boat had been installed that had been giving nothing but trouble, and was now used only for emergency vehicles. The local residents were greatly put out by the inconvenience, since it forced many of them to add an hour to their trips to Rio Vista and Isleton.

But the Garmin people hadn't gotten the word, and Sarah had blithely sent me there. If she sends me there in the future, I'll check with Caltrans first.

Part Three: Side Trips

The Curious Incident of the Bus in the Night-Time

This is a story about a VW bus that broke down. For once, it wasn't mine.

In 2009, as I've related, I installed a new engine in my bus. I wanted to make a shake-down trip within two hundred miles of home, and it turned out that a camping trip had been planned for that very weekend up near Twain, California, less than a hundred fifty miles from Sacramento. The trip went smoothly, and I arrived at the campsite in plenty of time to find a space and set up camp. That's when this story begins:

It is now evening. We are sitting around the campfire drinking wine and chatting away, wondering where some of our other people were (notably Joe and Peter, who were driving up in separate buses from the San Francisco area). We find out at about 10:30, when I hear the chuffle of an air-cooled engine coming down the hill into camp. It is Joe.

"We have a situation," he says. It turned out that Peter's 1970 bus, which has been immaculately restored to almost show-room condition, has broken down a few miles away from camp. The bus had simply died ... from full power to no power. It wouldn't even idle. Peter had had an experience like this before, and it turned out to be the points and condenser, two components of the ignition system that are usually reliable. Peter has told Joe that the area on the distributor where the condenser mounts seems to be unusually warm, supporting the theory that the condenser had gone bad.

Attempts to re-time the engine and swap out the condenser with a spare had been unsuccessful, Joe says. It so happened that when I replaced my distributor earlier that week, I threw the old one into my spares kit. So I propose to Joe that he and I take my spare distributor and install it in Peter's bus. (In case it turns out to be the coil, Regis also gives me the spare he carries in his bus.)

165

Joe and I head back in his bus to Peter, who by this time has the company of two California highway patrolmen. (He informs us later that they stopped to see what the trouble was, and make the obligatory check on every VW bus to ensure that it's not driven by hippies transporting vast quantities of dope. Since Peter could pass for a Mormon missionary, at least on the surface, their fears were instantly quelled, but they stayed with their lights flashing to give Peter some security on the mountain road.) While the patrolmen watch, we swap out the distributor and crank the engine a dozen times. No luck. We then put in the old distributor with another set of points and plugs and crank the engine another dozen times. No luck. We check the coil. It's working fine ... nice blue spark. All in all, we probably crank the engine for four or five dozen revolutions while testing various configurations of distributor, condenser, and points, with no result.

By now, it's after midnight. The cops want to resume their patrol. Peter tells them to call a tow truck to tow the bus down into the camp; after a night's sleep, we're sure to diagnose and fix the problem, but it's useless to try to do it now.

The tow truck finally arrives, and we arrive in camp sometime after 1:30 in the morning. As I go to sleep, I'm reviewing everything we did, but something's nagging at me ... something that I should have noticed, but missed somehow.

The next morning, I realize what it was. Like the Sherlock Holmes story about the silence of the dog in the night-time, the "curious incident" was the lack of something that should have been there. It occurs to me that after cranking the engine all those times, we should have been smelling gasoline fumes. But we weren't. If the fuel pump was indeed pumping fuel into the carburetor, and the carb was supplying the cylinders with fuel, and the fuel wasn't being burned, it had to be going somewhere. Perhaps the fuel never got to the cylinders in the first place, and we should be looking at the fuel delivery system. Last night, this had been checked only to the extent that we peered down the fuel filler pipe to verify that there was gas in the tank.

I mention this to Peter, but he's still convinced that it's an ignition problem. So is Joe, who says, "It isn't the fuel pump.

166

Fuel pumps never go bad." So they go through the same process they did last night, swapping pieces out and cranking the engine without success – and, they start to notice, without smelling fumes.

At this point, Peter's desperate enough to try anything, including listening to me. So he pulls the fuel line off the carburetor, holds a plastic cup under the end, and cranks the engine.

No gas.

OK, then, the gas line is plugged somewhere up the line, probably at either the fuel filter or the fuel pump. We switch out the filter. Still no gas. We take the top off the fuel pump to expose the filter screen built into the pump. It's clean.

The moment of truth comes when we re-assemble the fuel pump and pull the feed hose off it. There's lots of gas coming out of the hose, so we know that the fuel pump is well supplied. But when we crank the engine with the outflow hose pulled off the pump, we get squat. The fuel pump itself is bad. I can't help feeling a little smug at being proved right, a feeling I cherish since it happens so seldom.

We confirm this by trickling a little of the gas from the plastic cup directly down the throat of the carburetor. The car coughs and idles for a few seconds.

Now that the problem is diagnosed, the cure is simple: buy and install a new fuel pump. But now it's Saturday afternoon, the nearest big town is over an hour away, and what are the odds that they'll have a part for a forty-year-old car?

But Peter's luck holds. There's a smaller town, Quincy, that's only twenty-five miles up the road. It has a NAPA store, and the store has a fuel pump that fits Peter's bus. The reason the auto parts store has the pump is that there's still a big demand for it … it replaces the fuel pump on nearly every Volkswagen, bug or bus, made from the 1940s up to about 1974, when VW replaced generators with larger alternators that necessitated a lower-sitting fuel pump. Whenever VW re-designed a part, it did its best to make sure that that same part would fit as many previous models as possible. That famous design philosophy of backward compatibility has saved Peter's butt, as it has saved so many other people's.

Peter gets a ride to Quincy from Melissa in her borrowed Syncro, buys the new fuel pump, and returns. As we all watch in expectation, he installs the new pump and cranks the engine. It takes a while, because the pump has to fill itself, and the fuel filter, and the carburetor bowl with gas, but by and by the engine catches and idles like a champ. We break out celebratory bottles of wine while Joe and Peter do a victory lap around the campground.

****

As it happened, that fuel pump lasted less than a year, but it was long enough for Peter to obtain a kit for rebuilding his original pump. It's now six years later, and that rebuilt pump is still going strong. As for me, I bought a spare fuel pump from J. C. Whitney and carry it with the other spare parts. It may not be any better in quality than the one that Peter got in Quincy – such aftermarket parts do not have the most reliable track record – but I have long held the theory that if a breakdown happens, it will most likely involve a part that you don't have. Therefore, the more spare parts you carry, the less likely that you will need any of them. So I don't really know if the fuel pump is good, and I'm too lazy to actually test it, but I figure that its presence, like a magic talisman, will assure that my present fuel pump won't go bad.

So far, I've been right.

168

Buses By the Bridge

1: Buses (and one Sienna) By the Bridge 2009

As I explained elsewhere, my bus broke down as I was on my way to the West Coast's biggest VW bus show, known as Buses By The Bridge. I wasn't going to let this keep me from attending, so I threw some camping equipment into my Toyota Sienna and headed out, only a few hours behind schedule.

I stopped at a motel in Needles for the night, and grabbed breakfast at a nearby McDonald's. Then it was on to Lake Havasu City, which I reached by about noon. I would have been there a quarter of an hour earlier, but got off Arizona Route 95 too early, at the exit marked "London Bridge Road." London Bridge Road did eventually terminate at London Bridge, but by a circuitous route that led first through miles of undeveloped desert, then past hastily constructed residential areas with names like "Vista del Lago" and ""Desert Rose."

Once I got past the Lake Havasu State Recreational Area, though, I found my bearings and located the area where the event was to take place. I drove past the gate, turned onto McCullough Boulevard, and went in search of a supermarket and an internet connection. I found them both just off the road. After shopping for groceries for the weekend, I went to the Lake Havasu City Public Library, which had wireless Internet, after a fashion; it turned out to be even slower than dial-up, so I did nothing more than check my email there.

Returning to the gate, I paid my entrance fee and explained that while I was there, my bus wasn't. It turned out that I wasn't the only one who had mechanical problems en route; one party actually broke down about fifty miles away and arrived on site via flatbed truck, trusting that somebody there would have the ability to put their bus into working order by the end of the event. The people at the gate were quite apologetic in explaining to me that while I was welcome to camp, it would have to be in

169

the general parking area with the other RVs instead of where the buses were. I agreed completely.

After I parked the Sienna in the Parking Lot of Shame, I went looking for people I knew. The first acquaintance I found there turned out to be Justin, who regarded me with some surprise. He was one of the people I was to caravan down with, and the first person I called when I broke down and told him to proceed without me. "You made it!" he said. I filled him in on the story, and he told me that Damon had also broken down en route. Damon had the luxury of working for the Kombi Haus, though, and was able to borrow an engine from one of the shop buses, make the switch, and get back on the road after a delay of only a few hours. When I found them, they had already spread out some parts in front of their van for sale or swap, making themselves one of the approximately twenty vendors who ringed the "public square" at the heart of the encampment.

Buses By the Bridge is hosted by the London Bridge Bullis ("bulli" being the German word for what in the US is called the "microbus") as a charity event to raise funds for local youth activities and other charities. The money comes from entry fees, raffle tickets, and concessions of food and firewood run by local youth groups. The first event was in 1991, and except for some dormant years in the nineties, it's been a yearly event up to the present time, with no end in sight. Its organizers claim that it's the largest VW bus event in the country. I can believe it. In 2009, there were well over two hundred buses in attendance.

For most attendees, the feel was that of a reunion. Every year, bus owners had made the pilgrimage, greeted other returnees and caught up on each other's lives and rides. I didn't have this perspective, since it was my first time there and I don't make friends easily. But I could appreciate how bus-owners formed an extended family and treated you with cordiality if not friendship. My credentials were additionally suspect because I hadn't arrived in my bus, and therefore couldn't have the pleasure of pointing to it and saying, "That's mine over there." Justin Campbell and Bob Frith knew who I was, of course, and I was allowed admission into their camps without comment. But I

170

didn't really feel "of the body" and knew that I wouldn't until I had a bus to show them.

That isn't to say that people weren't friendly. In fact, it's easy to strike up conversations, and most of the kids run around without a great deal of parental supervision, since the parents trust the rest of the show-goers to be good people. On my first morning in the Parking Lot of Shame, a young girl on a bicycle pedaled up to me and started a conversation. "What are you having for breakfast?" she inquired.

"Oatmeal," I replied.

"Yay!" she cried, and pedaled off. I watched her go, and then watched another fellow pedal past me with a cat on his shoulders.

After my breakfast, I strolled around, took a lot of pictures and asked a lot of questions. Most of the bus owners were more than happy to talk about their buses. Even a simple question like "Is that engine stock?" would elicit discourses on the merits of stock vs. modified engines and elaborate explanations of the non-stock features of that particular engine. But these were knowledgeable people, and it was worth it to listen to them.

As I expected, there were those who thought that the only purpose of bus ownership was to painstakingly restore it to original condition, take it to shows, and collect the prizes. There were also those who thought nothing of modifying anything that could be modified ... engines, bodies, interiors, lighting ... and turning their buses into expressions of their personality. But most of the owners fell into a middle category, which respected the engineering of the original design and kept their own customizations to a minimum. They were likely to be apologetic about it, but it was obvious that they weren't losing sleep over their sins. This attitude made me feel a little better about my own modifications to George, which were guided by two aesthetic mandates: to design something so that it looked that it might have been stock, even if it wasn't, and where possible to make it reversible. This was more possible with things like roof racks, which could be removed without tools, than nose-mounted tire carriers, which left tell-tale holes in the front of the car.

171

During a lull in the festivities, I wandered over to the London Bridge, about a half a mile away from the showgrounds. This bridge is one of the local landmarks, having been shipped from its original location in London, England to Lake Havasu City, where it was intended to anchor a resort community. When I first visited there in 2000 or so, the area was thriving, but it now sported more than its share of boarded-up shops. Entire portions of it were fenced off, awaiting redevelopers who had so far failed to put up any money. There were plenty of empty buildings with ersatz Tudor facades, but they were padlocked. A large sign read "Future Development Now In Planning" and there were still a few shops open selling boat rides, sunglasses, tee shirts, and such. The shopkeepers were optimistic that good times would be back, but it was hard to see much evidence of progress.

The bridge itself seemed to be conspicuously out of place and time here, a relic of a culture far different from this sprawling desert community of retirees and tourists. I went over and gave the stones of the bridge a pat, as I had done when I first visited there. I'd written an article on the London Bridge years ago, and it still had a place in my heart.

My first visit was otherwise not a positive experience for me, as I looked too scruffy for the likes of the local constabulary, and they went out of their way to make sure that I did not stay long in their town. I assume that when harder times came to the city, the police force was no longer quite so eager to hustle what they considered undesirable elements out of town, as long as they spent money.

When Buses By the Bridge ended on Sunday, there was the sound of over two hundred buses firing up their air-cooled engines and warming up. The sound could have been that of a World War II airfield in England or France at the break of dawn, when squadrons of aircraft were readied for takeoff. I thought about how Reimspeiss,the designer of that engine, might have felt upon hearing that sound, and I wondered how Alfred Häsner might have felt if he'd known how esteemed his design was over half a century after he had created it.

I really didn't want to hit the road again right away, so I spent the night at the Lake Havasu recreation area's camping section. The next day, I made my way in leisurely fashion to San Bernadino, stopping at Quartzite to see if there was anything worth buying at the flea market there. (There wasn't.) After a night's sleep at a motel in San Berdoo, I traveled to Pacific Palisades to meet Jack McNeil, the previous owner of my bus.

2. Buses (Including George) by the Bridge 2010

In 2010, there are around 280 buses here, plus assorted beetles, Karmann Ghias, Things, and miscellaneous rear-engined VWs. This is not to mention a variety of other vehicles, but most of these aren't allowed into the show itself, and must remain in the general parking area.

This year, I'm with everybody else on the park's huge lawn. Much of the area has already been allocated to groups that have participated in the past, but I'm not affiliated with any of them, so I'm on my own. I was told that if you wanted to get a good spot, you should be at the gate by 6 a.m. I found this out the day before the show started, because I was part of the crew that helped the London Bridge Bullis set up the event, distributing trash cans. tables and benches, marking off the allocated areas with surveyor's tape, and flagging sprinkler heads so they won't be run over by the hundreds of cars in the show. To do this, I show up at 8 am and work until most of the set-up is completed, which is around 1 p.m.

Ronnie Feitelson, one of the spark plugs of the London Bridge Bullis (LBB), is there directing who goes where. He has a business in Lake Havasu City called Bustorations which supplies replacement parts for split-window buses, some of which are custom made for him. Last year, he described how his group works. "After so many years of doing this, it's just pretty well self-run. Everybody in our group's got their jobs to do and everybody does them. We have a little communication: 'Will you get this done? Did you get that done?' And when the day starts, everything's together." But now, the day before BBB 2010, things aren't exactly together. He's fretting that the portable toilets still haven't been delivered, and is on the cell phone to one of the other LBB members who's been assigned to track them down.

Most of the other set-up work has been done by this time, and the large mobile stage has been hauled in, leveled, and opened up. There is come concern that there might not be enough power to run the stage activities and still have some available for the campers, and Ronnie has to tell people not to expect that they'll be able to plug in. His attitude is brisk and businesslike, but he doesn't try to be diplomatic where he feels there's no point to it.

A reporter named Jackie Leatherman shows up from one of the local papers. Ronnie gives her a few minutes of his time, answering the usual questions. His relationship with the other local paper hasn't always been smooth, since he feels that they've dropped the ball both in publicizing the event and telling the public what it's for. He points out that it's not just a bunch of hippies camping out in buses; LBB has raised thousands and thousands of dollars for local charities directly and, by allowing other non-profits like the Boy Scouts and the Daytona Middle School to run food and firewood concessions, has fed even more money into these organizations. Ms. Leatherman promises that the *News-Herald* will tell the entire story. She writes notes down furiously in a small note-book and takes some pictures.

At one point, Ronnie is called away to deal with one of the innumerable details of the set-up, and she turns around to interview one of the other people standing by, who happens to be me. She asks me the basic questions one would expect: Why are you here? Which bus is yours? How did you get interested in buses? I told her the story of my cross-country trip in 1970, sharing a split-window camper with a handful of students. I then described how this event was different from most of the other VW shows I've attended. I remember telling her that what bonds VW enthusiasts together is that we share a lot of experiences, of which we still bear the scars.

I ask Ronnie if I could be allowed to camp that night with the Sacramento chapter of the London Bridge Bullis, who come down every year to set up and get an extra night of camping as a reward, but my name isn't on the list of those allowed to overnight, so back to the Windsor campground I go. I stayed there last year, after the show, and had the place pretty much to myself, but this year it's packed, due to the closure of two other

174

nearby state campgrounds. Fortunately, there are two large overflow parking lots and since VW campers don't take up much space, the rangers were able to pack another eighty cars comfortably there.

The next morning, I get up at 5 a.m., make coffee and some oatmeal, and am ready to roll by quarter of six. I drive the couple of miles to the BBB site. (The site is actually less than half a mile away from the campground and is usually connected by a road, but that road is blocked by a gate which will remain locked for the weekend.) When I arrive, I find that I am the thirty-fourth car in line. There's nothing to do for an hour or so, and I still don't feel very awake, so I fire up the propane stove and make another pot of coffee (one of the attractions of a camper is that you can do that whenever you want, without setting up a kitchen first.)

When the gate finally opens at around seven, there's light in the eastern sky. Many of the other arrivals have elected to camp in one of the allocated areas, so there's lots of space to choose from. I find a small spot just off the perimeter road, next to a group from the Portland area called the Wet Westies, who came down the night before and camped on some BLM land near the Lake Havasu City airport. I find that I know a few of them from Maupin last year, and make their re-acquaintance.

At some point, somebody hands me a newspaper. "You're a celebrity, dude," he says. It's the Lake Havasu *Today's News-Herald.* Jackie's story is the lead article, and it begins with our interview. Her story is pretty accurate, and does mention the fund-raising, although my quote about "common scars" comes out as "common scares." But that works, too.

As the event progresses, it becomes clear that there are far more buses than there were last year (I would find out that the unofficial count was 280, up from last year's 240 or so). I also noticed far fewer vendors. Otherwise, there's not much difference between the two events. It's still a family-oriented event, with lots of things to do for the children. There's one of those big inflatable playgrounds, there's a bean-bag tossing competition, there are coloring contests. "Every kid gets to be a winner. Everybody gets a prize," John "VW" Howard told me when I interviewed him after

175

last year's show. "People can come here and know their kids are safe."

John Howard has been around VW buses for over forty-five years now. He is an affable man who talked to me in a stream of broken, unfinished sentences, as if each succeeding thought was elbowing the previous one aside. It might have been the pressure of the show (he usually needs a day or two to decompress), or it may have just been the way he talks all the time.

"I bought my first bus when I was sixteen and it was 1964," he told me. "It was in southern California, and I was a surfer. We used it every day for surfing, and I had a Volkswagen bus ever since. I've never been without one since 1964. Almost 45 years now, almost? I've gotten through hundreds of them. Selling them, trading them, fixing them up..."

I'd asked him if he'd gotten attached to any of them. "There's been maybe three of them out of all the hundreds," he said. "I had a Benz crew cab. I had that in the early nineties and nobody even knew what they were and they didn't want them. And then I had a double-door barn door bus '54 panel with the double door on both sides and then I had a twenty-one-window sunroof deluxe bus. And now I've got this high-roof one ... I've been looking for a high roof forever and I finally picked that one up. So that one will be a keeper. I'll never get rid of that one. And all my friends got a bet that, well, I've said it before, but .... But my wife likes it 'cause we go camping, and she can stand up inside it and change clothes and stuff, and that's what she likes about it. That'll be a keeper for sure, that one.

"All of us could have retired if we'd kept our buses, now with the money they're going for," he continued. "But we were trying to add it up, a couple months ago we were sitting there talking, and in the forty-five years, it's been about four hundred buses I've gone through."

John has one other claim to fame among VW bus enthusiasts: he was the one that first cut out wheel wells for oversize tires, back in the sixties when he was surfing. In doing so, he started a trend. "In those days, that '64 panel I bought, my very first bus, I had the wheel wells cut out within two hours of getting it home. The reason being, we put those grooved farm

176

implement tires on them. We had to have a guy widen the rims for us, and the reason was that in those days, you could actually drive on the beach at Huntington Beach and also [Bolsa] Chica Beach, and you needed those tires to get on the sand. That was the main reason I did that, and all my group of surfer dudes did. And we went down to Mexico and those sand beaches. And those farm implement tires, they were only rated for forty or fifty miles an hour, but you could let the air down to three or four pounds and you could go anywhere. And that was the reason I cut so many of those for me and friends and, you know, everybody had it. It was the first thing you did – cut the wheel wells so you could go get down to the beaches."

After a while, we get around to talking about the event. "We orientate it as a family event, and we police it, and we don't allow riffraff," he added. "We kick them out. At ten o'clock we make it the quiet time. That's it." John also pointed out how the park's proximity to Lake Havasu City has been a boon. "There's a hotel right across the street, and that's helped, too, because a lot of wives don't like to camp in buses, but they like the event, and they bring the kids. So it's real convenient, and they can walk here."

John Howard hosted the first Buses By the Bridge in 1991, and has worked on every one of them since then. That first one was held in April, on an undeveloped lot in Crazy Horse Campground, on the island connected to Lake Havasu City by the London Bridge. Eighteen buses showed up, mostly locals. The event was technically under the auspices of the North East Association of Transporter Owners (NEATO) which provided the insurance and some publicity. The event garnered praise from its participants, but it was a strain for one person to put on, and so John took a break that ended up lasting four years.

In the meantime, the NEATO members in the area had formed their own chapter of the club, the London Bridge Bullis, and it was to them that John turned for help the next time around. Ronnie Feitelson was one of the driving forces behind LBB, and at first, John and Ronnie didn't get along, but they put their differences aside in 1995 to put together BBB II, and have jointly put on every show since then. "At first, it was all split buses allowed down here," Matt Adragna recalled. "But we realized that's no fun if a group of people come in who are bay windows or Vanagons and split windows, and they want to camp together." Over the years, there has been a greater number of post 1967 buses, and in 2009, they outnumbered the splitties for the first time.

John points out with some pride that over the years, the show has put close to eighty thousand dollars into the coffers of local charities (the same point that Ronnie was making with the newspaper reporter). Over the years, BBB has become its own legal entity as a limited-liability corporation with non-profit status, and now provides its own insurance and logistical support. It still relies heavily on the dozen or so members of the LBB to make sure everything happens on time. Matt is one of them; he's been at every one since the second. He tells me the story of how he met John: "He actually lived two blocks away, and I'd never even met him. Then one day I was having a garage sale, and had some Volkswagen stuff out there for sale, and here comes John Howard. He scoops up all my VW stuff. It turns out he's a VW enthusiast, and he lived around the corner from me, and I never knew him."

John and Matt became good friends, and they decided to do a second BBB in 1996. It was then that they decided to move the date from April to January. "When we set the date again, we looked around and there were already shows in April," John told me. "We got to talking about it, and we wanted to be the first show of the year. In January, there's fairly decent weather, and that really made a difference, getting people out of the cold." So it was decided to hold it on the weekend of Martin Luther King Day. "A lot of people don't get the day off, but a lot of postal workers and school teachers love it, because it gives them the extra day to get home and travel, so they don't need to take as much vacation time."

Until 2016, the biggest BBB was its tenth anniversary, in 2006, when 312 buses showed up. By that time, they were no longer at Crazy Horse Campground, having moved the show to the Windsor recreation area in 1999. Since then, attendance has varied from between two and three hundred buses. Matt thinks that that's about right. It could conceivably go bigger (Windsor Park could probably accommodate 350 buses without undue strain) and longer (people have been clamoring to extend it by a day), but at its present size, the event puts enough pressure on the LBB. To make it bigger, they'd have to turn its management over to a promoter, and that might change the character of the show in ways they'd just as soon avoid. Much of the event's allure is its low-key feeling. It feels more like a family reunion than an auto show.

There are only a few "official" activities. Some of them are the bean-bag tosses and the coloring contests for the kids. Others are raffles. Vendors from all over the country contribute prizes ranging from hats and tee shirts to entire engines and transmissions, so the raffles are well-attended. I don't win anything, although a ticket that I dropped and lost turns out to have been a winner. In 2009, the winner of the engine didn't need it, so he auctioned it off right then and there. And then he donated a thousand dollars of the proceeds to BBB. (John Howard tells me later that the fellow who bought the engine really needed it. His engine blew on the way to the event and he ended up arriving at the park on a trailer, confident that somehow or another, the collection of bus lovers would make sure he left under his own power.)

But most of the time is unstructured, and people just schmooze. They see old friends, and make new ones. They compare engines and body styles, and trade sources and tips. Every type of bus enthusiast is represented. You'll see pristine buses, lovingly restored to showroom condition and trailered in from afar, parked next to wildly customized ones with dropped frames, safari windows, glitter paint, and monster engines. And right next to them you'll see beat-up buses like mine, whose only purpose in life is to be used as campers and daily drivers. It's all good — they're all buses. When evening falls, people retire to their own areas to cook dinner, drink beer, and bring out musical instruments for impromptu jam sessions.

One of the big attractions in 2010 is Walter, the Giant Bus, a commercial truck whose body has been reworked to vaguely resemble a quadruple scale VW split-window microbus (it started

179

out as a drop-side pickup, but its owners eventually decided on the Samba look). It's easily the tallest vehicle on site, and there is a steady stream of people who snap pictures of the event from its observation deck.

In the past thirty years or so, here's been an odd reversal in who owns what sort of bus. When I got into the game, the people without money were the ones with the split-window buses, and the people with money drove the later-model "bay window" buses. Now the positions have been reversed, with the split-faces becoming so collectible, yet so much harder to keep on the road for lack of parts, that only those with lots of spare cash can afford to buy and maintain them. I mention this to John at one point, and he agrees. "The biggest change is the Vanagons and the Eurovans coming in, just like you've seen, too. Another change, which we're starting to get back in, is we're starting to get young kids back in now, because they can afford them. They can't afford a street rod, the street machines are so expensive, but they can buy a Volkswagen cheap, and drive it while they're working on it. We've got people coming back now and, gosh, their kids are almost ready to drive now. The babies were a month old, or two months old, when they were here at some of the first ones."

3. Buses By the Bridge XX (2016)

I made it to Buses By the Bridge in 2016, and I made it back, too. The story of that trip touches on so many of the themes of this book that it could serve as a final chapter. There's the impromptu mechanicking and the recurring lesson that no matter how well-planned you think your journey is, it may well end up being a different trip than the one you expected. And there's the realization that you're part of a passionate community of VW bus owners and the people who keep them on the road, helping where they can and offering moral support when they can't.

This year's Buses By the Bridge was BBB XX, the twentieth Buses By the Bridge, and it drew over five hundred VW buses from all over the country, not to mention over a hundred other vehicles and a few hundred people who day-tripped to the event. There was no way I would miss this one. In fact, the only one I'd missed since I got George was in 2012, when a leg infection made long-distance traveling out of the question.

The week before BBB XX, I'd done a tune-up on the bus to prepare it for the trip. I'd changed the oil, done a valve adjustment (during which I replaced the valve cover gaskets), and checked the timing and tire pressures. I then drove to Kombi Haus, where Wally did a compression test and gave it a general look-over to see if there were any issues that needed to be dealt with before the trip. He recommended that I change the spark plug wires, distributor cap, and rotor. I bought the parts and installed them the next day, confident that the bus would give me hundreds and hundreds of miles of trouble-free service. As usual, I was wrong.

The first incident happened at a rest area near Tulare, California. I got out to use the restroom and stretch my legs. Then I got back into the bus and turned the key. Nothing. Not even a click from the starter. All the warning lights came on, so I knew that it wasn't a massive electrical failure. Well, what are you supposed to do? You take a flashlight and roll under the bus to take a look at the starter and its electrical connections. It usually doesn't do anything to help the situation, in my experience, but at least you can say you did something before calling the tow truck. So that's what I did, and to my amazement, I found the problem right away: a broken wire to the solenoid. I got out my crimping tool and the appropriate terminal connection and was on the road again within ten minutes. I cruised on down the road, smug in my ability to use my mechanical skills to avert disaster. There must be celestial beings who watch out for that sort of thing, and are poised to deploy countermeasures. In this case, they waited for about two hundred miles, and struck.

As I neared Barstow, the generator light came on. It was the first trouble I'd had with the charging system in five years, and I figured that by this time, there wasn't much that it could throw at me that I couldn't cope with. But since it was past sunset, I decided to spend the night at a motel and try to locate a garage in the morning.

The next day, I called several garages and found out that not one of them was willing to work on an air-cooled Volkswagen. It was up to me to get this fixed. So I found a parking lot in front of a fenced-in, boarded-up abandoned business in which to work. (Such parking lots and abandoned storefronts are nearly as common in Barstow as stop signs.) Since the light came on quickly and brightly, I figured that it was probably the voltage regulator, so I swapped it out for a spare I was carrying — the same spare I saved after my last go-around with a charging problem.

No difference. The light still came on.

I found that there was a mechanic in Hesperia who would be able to look at the car. Hesperia was about forty miles away, and I made it down there with the generator light leering at me malevolently the whole time. The mechanic turned out to be Joel Mohr, the owner of Mohr Performance. Joel had begun his career in VWs in a shop that swapped out engines for people who needed to pass the smog test but weren't willing to put the effort or money to get their engines legal (or who preferred to keep them non-stock). But Joel saw that there was a limited future in this sort of work, so he found steady work elsewhere as a machinist. After getting laid off one time too many, he got back into Volkswagens and opened a shop specializing in modifications for racing and off-road cars. His shop was a busy one, so I was glad that he had the time to look at my problem.

The first thing he noticed was that the generator brushes were worn down almost to the limit. This was significant because, as the brushes wore down, less pressure was exerted on them by the retaining springs. This in turn degraded the contact between the brushes and the generator's armature. He gave me a set of almost-new brushes from a generator he'd replaced with the more trouble-free alternator that was available for these cars. I managed to get one brush installed, but the other one resisted my best efforts, even after two hours of labor. But was one generator brush enough to get me going again? The only way to find out was to start the car and see what happened.

182

I started the car. The generator light went out. Hallelujah! I was on the road again!

But after about fifteen minutes of blissful driving, the light went back on. Well, maybe I had enough juice in the battery to get to the Lake Havasu State Park campground, where I'd booked a campsite with electricity. I always carry a puny two-ampere charger with the rest of my tool kit. If I could get there, I could plug in the charger and re-charge the battery overnight. The park was about two hundred miles away from Barstow, with about half that distance driving in the dark with my headlights on. Well, if I ran out of juice, I could always call Triple-A and have the bus towed to the campsite, or to a garage in Lake Havasu City, or to the show ground itself, which was about a mile away. I pressed on.

Along the way, I met Justin Campbell of Kombi Haus, who was going to the same show, and we talked about the problem. By that time, we were about twenty miles from Lake Havasu City, and the battery seemed to be holding up just fine. I was actually wondering if there hadn't been a problem with the charging system at all, and it was merely the indicator light itself that was malfunctioning. Justin said that it was possible, and that there were ways to check that once I'd arrived at the show.

As a matter of fact, it turned out to be the charging system that was bad. The battery lasted just long enough to get me to the campground before it died. Joe Ehrlich and his girlfriend Corey were already there, and they towed my bus to my campsite. We pushed it in, I hooked up the charger, and shared a glass of wine with them before turning in. The only food I'd had all day were a McDonald's egg breakfast and some strips of pork jerky, but I was too tired to even consider making myself dinner.

The next morning, the battery was charged enough to get me back on the road, but the red light was still on. We were at the main gate of Buses by the Bridge before sunrise, only to find over a hundred cars in line ahead of us. I toasted some Pop-Tarts on my camp stove and made a pot of coffee, which I shared with a gentleman from Mexico. Mercifully, the organizers opened the gates two hours earlier than planned, and after a worrisome hour of stop-and-start driving, with me occasionally shutting the

183

engine off and then re-starting it, we were through the gate and looking for a campsite. The place I'd intended to camp at was already occupied, so we found another place on the other side of the show grounds.

I awarded myself the rest of the day off, and refused to think about my ailing bus. The rest of that day was devoted to the things that I came to the event for: looking up old friends, inspecting the various things that people were putting up for sale on tables in front of their buses, and admiring buses that had been meticulously restored, at a cost of thousands and thousands of dollars. The large, grassy lawn in front of a portable stage called the Pearl Bailey Showmobile had been kept clear as a sort of community town square. Later on, bounce houses would be set up for the kids, and hot air balloons would be launched from there, but now it was just a large open space for folks to ride their bikes, fly kites, and toss their frisbees around. Joe and Corey fed me dinner, and we sat around talking for a while. But it had already been a long day for us, and we retired early.

The next day, when the sun had taken the chill off the morning, I opened the rear engine hatch went to work. I can't count the number of people who saw me there and came over to offer advice, spare parts, a beer, or just moral support. While I didn't need any of that, it was reassuring to see how people reacted to my plight. There's a feeling with shows like this that, even if you are towed in, folks won't rest until you can leave under your own power. I was sure that I was in the best of company in situations like this. Days afterward, people would stop me as I walked around and ask me if I needed their help in getting the problem sorted out, even though I'd never met them before and didn't even know their names, nor they mine. I suspected that they'd all been where I was at one time or another, broken down far from home and ready to accept all the help they could get.

After another two hours, I finally got the second generator brush out. The generator brush spring came out with it, to my consternation. That spring is a bitch to get back in, because you have to find a way to compress it and keep it tensioned as you

184

slip it in to its narrow opening in the generator. I consulted the official service manual, which gave no help whatsoever. Then I pulled out the Idiot Book. John Muir described how another owner had solved the problem by wrapping the spring with fine copper wire, installing the spring, and then cutting the wire. "I haven't tried it," Muir wrote, "but it sounds possible." Well, it was possible. I didn't have any fine copper wire, but I did have some stainless steel tie wire and used that, and the generator brush spring was installed after another vexatious half-hour. Then I installed the new brush and screwed it into place. I turned the ignition on and started the car.

The generator light didn't go out.

Well, I thought, I've done everything I could. I've changed the brushes and the voltage regulator, so it had to be the generator itself that's at fault. Changing the generator involves removing the engine from the car, which would have been difficult enough if I was home but was pretty much unthinkable when I'm six hundred miles away. (Yes, I know that I'd done it before when I was on the road, but that was when I was less than half my present age. And I didn't have the necessary jacks at hand this time.)

I had two options. First, I could have the generator overhauled, but that might take days. There were rebuilt generators to be had, but they were rare and expensive, and it would have to be shipped to Lake Havasu City. The second option was to have have the generator replaced with an alternator, as I've mentioned earlier. Joe was firmly in favor of the latter option; he'd had the generator in his bus replaced with an alternator, and he'd never regretted it. The cost would be about the same.

But I would have to find a garage in Lake Havasu City that could do the work. I turned to John Howard, one of the show's two chief organizers, for help, and he referred me to Ronnie Feitelson, the other chief organizer. Ronnie owns a garage in the city and he not only could do the work but actually had the very alternator in stock that I needed. He'd brought it to the show for somebody else, he said, but that person hadn't shown, so it was mine if I wanted it. I did want it, and made arrangements to have my bus at his shop when it opened on Monday.

When the show ended on Sunday, Joe and Corey escorted me back to the campground at Lake Havasu State Park. Although the campground was full, I was given a spot in their overflow area, and I assured Joe and Cory that if my battery died again overnight, I could get Triple-A to tow me to Ronnie's garage in the morning. I sent them off on their travels, took a shower, made some dinner, and read a book by the light of a kerosene lantern, since I was saving as much of the battery's charge as I could.

The bus indeed had enough juice the next morning to get me to the garage. Ronnie found me waiting for him when he arrived to open the shop, and his mechanic Jerry told me to pull into the back entrance of the shop. Jerry did most of the actual work, but Ronnie checked on him from time to time while operating the main core of his business, which was selling replacement sheet metal used in restoring old bus bodies. In between telephone calls, I was able to chat with him and learn how he had ended up with such a successful niche enterprise.

George at Ronnie's Garage

Like John Howard, Ronnie was from southern California. He had started out in landscaping, eventually building up a successful business with an impressive payroll and vehicle fleet, which he sold. Then he turned to restoring Porsches, acquiring a reputation for meticulous work. He and his family moved to Lake Havasu City, and he began to sell the VW restoration parts for which he is now one of the principal providers. "I've got the No. 3 (parts shop) in the country," he told a local newspaper in 2014. "Bus parts are a huge on-line business, too."

Ronnie has a brusque, no-nonsense demeanor that often turns people off. But as he described what sort of charities Buses By the Bridge was supporting, I got to see another side of him, one involved in making his community a better place by providing support for poor children, battered women, and veterans. His participation in Buses By the Bridge has been unwavering, and he is constantly fighting to preserve his concept of inclusiveness and family-friendliness in the face of those who would try to tamper with the show's format. For example, when a proposal was made to turn over the show's large open "town square" area to more camping, he replied that the public space was a vital part of the show's success, and that if it was reduced, he would no longer help organize it. And he was right about the importance of that open space, I think; one of the things one notices is how that area is used for the "bounce houses" for the kids, seating for the raffles, and as a play area for all the attendees — not to mention the occasional launch of a hot-air balloon, which is always a crowd-pleaser.

The alternator installation ended up taking all day, because he and Jerry found a few other issues that had to be dealt with ... cracks in the rubber intake manifold joints, a variety of nuts and bolts and fittings that had shaken loose in the past few years, and so on. Ronnie had quoted me a price for the job based on about five hours of labor, but the job ended up about two hours longer than planned. He was going to stick to his original estimate, but I happily paid him a bit more than that, and felt that I owed him even more. I asked him if, instead of re-writing the bill yet again, I could just make a hundred-dollar contribution to the London Bridge Bullis towards the expenses of next year's show. He smiled and agreed, saying that he'd actually prefer to have it done that way.

I was able to get out of Lake Havasu City by sunset. All my troubles were behind me, right? Well, not really. On the way home, the oil pressure light started flickering when I was about a mile away from a rest area just west of Needles, California. As I coasted into the rest stop, the flicker became a solid red glow.

I got out a flashlight and investigated. The two hoses that connect the engine to an external oil filter were dripping with oil, leading me to think that, when they were re-connected as the engine was installed, they hadn't been tightened down enough. I got out some wrenches and rolled under the bus. The fittings were as tight as could be. I noticed that there was a lot of oil on the heater box just below the valve cover on the left side, as well as on the engine mount. Could there be a leak somewhere else?

I started the engine again. Shining the light on the valve cover, I noticed a steady drip of oil there. That was the problem: the valve cover gasket, which I'd installed after adjusting the valves the previous week, had slipped off off the rim of the head just enough to create a gap through which the oil was seeping. I'd lost almost all the oil in the engine. The leak certainly hadn't been there when I was working on the engine over the weekend, and it wasn't there when Ronnie and Jerry removed and replaced the engine. It was just another reminder of the eternal truth that things happen when they happen, and I could count myself lucky that it happened just when I was approaching a rest area. (I later found out that this sort of thing happens once in a while, for no apparent reason, and that the gasket glue I'd used was no longer recommended by my friends at Kombi Haus.)

And I was lucky that this was something I could fix on the spot. I had a spare gasket, which I installed. Then I found the quart and a half of oil that I'd stored one of the rear cabinets for just such emergencies. I poured it into the engine and started it up. No leaks. The generator debacle had sorely tested my faith in my ability to fix things, but I felt a measure of self-confidence returning as I headed down the road. I couldn't pass every test, but I could still pass a few of the easier ones.

Stopping at Ludlow, I bought another quart of oil from the Chevron station and poured that in, too, which brought the oil level to full. At the WalMart in Barstow, I bought two more quarts of oil to replenish my emergency stock and made it home the next day without further drama.

And the day after that, I mailed out a check for a hundred dollars, made out to London Bridge Bullis.

Acknowledgements

This book would not have been possible without the help of several friends, who caught several errors in the manuscript and pointed out areas where I hadn't been clear. Special mention goes to Joe Ehrlich, Alf Knoll, and Adam McDonald for applying their eagle eyes to my writings and finding innumerable misspellings. My brother, Joe LaTorre, also took the time to check some of the facts in the book, correcting me where I'd drawn the wrong conclusions from the literature.

I'd also like to thank Matt Adragna, Ronnie Feitelson, John Howard, Jack McNeil, Jewel Mehlman, and Jewel's daughter Felicia for allowing me to interview them for this book.

When I started this book, I thought I knew all that I needed to know about Volkswagen buses. I soon learned otherwise, and am grateful to Justin Campbell, Colin Kellogg, Mike "the Bus Whisperer" Fernandez, and many, many other people for their technical expertise and their willingness to share their knowledge with me.

And I owe special thanks to my wife Debra for so many things: casting her critical editorial eye on the copy, helping me with this book's formatting, putting up with me when the bus gave me trouble, allowing me to take extended trips without her, and generally being my reason to come back home.

Photo Credits:

All photographs are by the author except for page 4, which was taken by Margie Weigel, and pages 54 and 56, which were taken by Robin Gann.

Made in the USA
San Bernardino, CA
16 October 2016